# SHIN NIHONGO NO KISO I

## GRAMMATICAL NOTES IN ENGLISH

新日本語の基礎Ⅰ 文法解説書 英語版

# SHIN NIHONGO NO KISO I

## GRAMMATICAL NOTES
## IN ENGLISH

新日本語の基礎I 文法解説書 英語版

(財)海外技術者研修協会 編著

**THE ASSOCIATION FOR OVERSEAS TECHNICAL SCHOLARSHIP (AOTS)**

3A Corporation

Shoei Bldg., 6-3, Sarugaku-cho 2-chome, Chiyoda-ku, Tokyo 101-0064, Japan

©1992 by the Association for Overseas Technical Scholarship (AOTS)

First published in Japan by 3A Corporation 1992

ISBN4-906224-69-5 C0081
Printed in Japan

# PREFACE

This book is a revised edition of **NIHONGO NO KISO I Grammatical Notes in English**, which has been prepared to accompany the recently completed textbook, **SHIN NIHONGO NO KISO I**. **SHIN NIHONGO NO KISO I** is carefully designed to introduce sentence patterns in order of difficulty; beginning with simple structures and advancing towards more complex ones. This will enable the learners to study them systematically. Although **Renshū A** (Drill A) of each lesson explains the newly introduced basic sentence patterns with illustrations, the Grammatical Notes are to assist the learners further by giving a brief description of important grammatical points.

In preparing this book, we have tried to discuss sentence patterns and important points in each lesson without using grammarian's terminology. As this book has been compiled as a grammar for beginners, highly technical details or grammatical discussions have not been included.

This book will be most effective when used in conjunction with **SHIN NIHONGO NO KISO I** and its translation, either under the instruction of Japanese language teachers or for students' self-study.

I would like to express my thanks to Keiko Mihara for translating and Motoko Tsuchiya and Nicholas McNeill for checking this edition.

April 1992

The Association for Overseas Technical Scholarship

# CONTENTS

Notations used to show word-categories are as follows:

N          noun (**meishi**)

           e. g. **tsukue**        *desk*

           **kenshūsei**          *trainee*

A          i-adjective (**i-keiyōshi**)

           e. g. **atsui**         *hot*

           **takai**              *high*

Na         **na**-adjective (**na-keiyōshi**)

           e. g. **shizuka-na**    *quiet*

Adv        adverb (**fukushi**)

           e. g. **taihen**        *very*

           **hakkiri**            *clearly*

V          verb (**dōshi**)

           e. g. **kakimasu**      *write*

           **yomimasu**           *read*

P          particle (**joshi**)

           e. g. **ga**, **o**, **no**

1. A predicate always comes at the end of a sentence.
2. A verb has no inflection for person, gender or number.
3. There are no articles in Japanese.
4. Most of the nouns have no plural form.
5. A particle is placed at the end of a word or a sentence to indicate the relationship between the words in a given context or to add various meanings.
6. A subject and an object are often omitted if they may be understood from the context without being stated explicitly.
7. There are plain and polite styles in Japanese; one is chosen over the other in daily conversation depending on circumstances.

## Ⅱ. Japanese Script

There are three kinds of letters used in the Japanese writing system: **Kanji** (Chinese characters), **Hiragana** and **Katakana** (Japanese syllabaries).

Written Japanese is a hybrid writing system where **Kanji**, **Hiragana** and **Katakana** are combined to write a sentence. Foreign names and loan-words are written in **Katakana**. In addition to the above three types of letters, **Rōmaji** (roman letters) is sometimes used, but only on signboards or on signs specifically put up for foreigners; it is not used in ordinary writing.

1. **Rōmaji**      **Nihon-go**      *Japanese language*
   **Hiragana**    にほんご          *Japanese language*
   **Katakana**    ニホンゴ          *Japanese language*
   **Kanji**       日本語            *Japanese language*

2. **Watashi wa Kenshū   Sentā  de Nihon-go  o  benkyō-shimasu.**
   わたし  は  研修  センター  で  日本語  を  勉強  します。
   □     ○   ○    △      □   ○     □   ○    □

   *I study Japanese at the Kenshu Center.*

   ○ ... **Kanji**
   □ ... **Hiragana**
   △ ... **Katakana**

In this textbook roman letters are used for the sake of convenience for short-term Japanese learners.

1

## Ⅲ. Pronunciation of Japanese

**Japanese syllables**

The Japanese syllabary is shown on the first page of the textbook, **SHIN NIHON-GO NO KISO I**.

A typical Japanese syllable consists of a vowel, or a consonant plus a vowel. Exceptions will be described later.

### 1. Vowels (boin)

#### 1) Short vowels

Japanese short vowels should be pronounced clearly.

**a** is pronounced like 'a' in 'father'. (But it is shorter)

**i** is pronounced like 'i' in 'machine'.

**u** is pronounced like 'u' in 'roof'. (But it is shorter)

**e** is pronounced like 'e' in 'pet'. (But it is shorter)

**o** is pronounced like 'o' in 'horse'. (But it is shorter)

#### 2) Long vowels

Some vowels in Japanese are lengthened and pronounced as long vowels, and a vowel carries a different meaning depending on whether it is pronounced long or short. It is, therefore, important to distinguish between short and long vowels when listening to and speaking Japanese.

In romanized transcription (**Rōmaji**), a long vowel is marked by a bar above the letter as shown below, except for the long vowels of **i** and **e** which are written as **ii** and **ei**. Other exceptions are **ee** (*yes*) and **onēsan** (*elder sister*).

| short vowel : | a | i | u | e | o |
|---|---|---|---|---|---|
| long vowel : | ā | ii | ū | ē, ei | ō |

|  |  |  |  |  |
|---|---|---|---|---|
| yuki | *snow* | ; | yūki | *courage* |
| ojisan | *uncle* | ; | ojiisan | *grandfather* |
| heya | *room* | ; | heiya | *open field* |

### 2. Consonants (shi-in)

#### 1) Sound of n

**n** is a consonant, but it constitutes one syllable. **n** is pronounced differently according to the sound that follows it; no matter how it may be pronounced, the sound of **n** does not affect the meaning of the word of which it is a part.

*[ n ]* before **t**, **d**, and **n**; on̲na, un̲dō, an̲tei

*[ m ]* before **m**, **p**, and **b**; bun̲mei, san̲po, shin̲bun

*[ ŋ ]* in cases other than above; san̲kai, kan̲gaeru

2 ) **Sound of g**

When **g** comes at the beginning of a word, it is pronounced 〔 g 〕, and in other cases, it is usually pronounced as 〔 ŋ 〕, except in **go** ( 5 ) where it is always pronounced as 〔 g 〕. Recently some Japanese do not differentiate between 〔 g 〕 and 〔 ŋ 〕 and use 〔 g 〕 in any case.

3 ) **Double Consonants**

Some consonants such as **k**, **t**, **s** and **p** occur as double consonants. For instance, in **otto**, [-t-] between [o] and [to] indicates that the sound is suspended between [o] and [to] for the length of one mora (the length of one beat). Listen to the tape carefully and practise until you fully acquire a sense of a mora length.

| | | |
|---|---|---|
| oto | *sound* | (**o-to**: 2 moras) |
| otto | *husband* | (**o-t-to**: 3 moras) |
| shite imasu | *be doing something* | (**shi-te**) |
| shitte imasu | *to know* | (**shi-t-te**) |

4 ) **Consonant + ya, yu, yo or sh, ch + vowel**

Such sounds as **kya**, **kyu**, **kyo**, **gya**, **gyu**, **gyo**, **sha**, **shi**, **shu**, **she**, and **sho** are counted as one mora sound.

| | | |
|---|---|---|
| kyaku | *guest* | (**kya-ku** : 2 moras) |
| kiyaku | *agreement* | (**ki-ya-ku** : 3 moras) |

3

3 . **Length of a syllable and accent**

1 ) The length of a syllable in Japanese is almost always constant (one mora), except for long-vowel syllables and double-consonant syllables which are twice as long as other syllables (2 moras).

2 ) There is little stress accent used in Japanese words; instead there is pitch accent. As shown below, a different pitch accent type indicates difference in meaning. Pitch accent types vary in different localities and in complex words.

{ ha⌐shi *bridge*    { ki⌐ru *to wear*
{ ha⌐shi *chopsticks*   { ki⌐ru *to cut*

4 . **Devoicing of the vowels i and u**

The vowels **i** and **u** are devoiced when they occur between the voiceless consonants of **k**, **s**, **t**, **p** and **h**, or in **desu** and **masu**.

| | |
|---|---|
| tsúkue | *desk* |
| súki | *to like* |
| kíkimasú | *to listen* |
| desú | *to be* |

# Lesson 1

### 1. Noun [N]

In Japanese nouns do not change their forms for number (singular/plural) or for gender (masculine/feminine) with only a few exceptions.

### 2. Particles [P] ... wa, mo, ka, etc.

In Japanese a grammatical relation between words or between phrases is indicated by particles which come after words or phrases. There are various particles and their uses vary widely; details will be given for each particle in the relevant sections.

1) | N  wa |

wa indicates what the speaker is going to talk about or the topic of a sentence.

    **Watashi wa kenshūsei desu.**    *I am a trainee.*

2) | N  mo |

Like **wa**, **mo** indicates that the word or phrase to which it is attached is the topic; **mo** is used, however, when the same thing or event is already presupposed to be true.

    **Tanaka-san wa Nihon-jin desu.**    *Mr. Tanaka is a Japanese.*
    **Kimura-san mo Nihon-jin desu.**    *Miss Kimura is also a Japanese.*

3) | Sentence  ka | ... 1

An interrogative sentence is made by putting **ka** at the end of a sentence. The interrogative sentence ends with a rising intonation.

    **Anata wa kenshūsei desu ka.**↗    *Are you a trainee?*

4) | N  no  N | ... 1

**no** connects a noun with another noun and the former modifies the latter. **no** in this case denotes a possessive. For other uses of **no**, see Lesson 2 and Lesson 3.

    **Watashi wa Tōkyō-denki no kenshūsei desu.**
    *I am a trainee of Tokyo Denki Co., Ltd.*

## 3. desu

1 ) **desu** is used at the end of a sentence ending with a noun or an adjective and indicates judgement or assertion. It also conveys that the speaker is being polite towards the listener (see Lesson 20).

2 )
| affirmative | **desu** |
|---|---|
| negative | **dewa arimasen** |

   * **ja arimasen** may be used in place of **dewa arimasen** in daily conversation.

## 4. -san

In Japanese -**san** is attached after the listener's or a third party's name to show respect to that person.  -**san** should never be used when the speaker is referring to his own name.

| | |
|---|---|
| **Watashi wa Kimura desu.** | *I am Kimura.* |
| **Anata wa Tanaka-san desu ka.** | *Are you Mr. Tanaka?* |

| | |
|---|---|
| **Tanaka Haruo** | full name |
| **Tanaka** | family name |
| **Haruo** | given name |

In Japan either the full name or the family name is used in referring to a person's name.  The given name alone is used only among very close friends or within a family.

## 5. Interrogative sentence ... 1

There are three kinds of interrogative sentences in Japanese; here we will learn the following two kinds.

1 ) Interrogative sentence with the particle **ka** at the end of it.

| | |
|---|---|
| **Anata wa kenshūsei desu ka.** | *Are you a trainee?* |
| ···**Hai, kenshūsei desu.** | ···*Yes, I am a trainee.* |
| ···**Iie, kenshūsei dewa arimasen.** | ···*No, I'm not a trainee.* |

In answering to this kind of question, make sure to add **Hai** *yes* or **Iie** *no*.  If you fail to do so, you might sound impolite.

2 ) Interrogative sentence with an interrogative.

| | |
|---|---|
| **Ano hito wa <u>dare</u> desu ka.** | *Who is he?* |
|   interrogative | |
| ···**Rao-san desu.** | ···*He is Mr. Rao.* |

Position of interrogatives
In English an interrogative word always comes at the beginning of a sentence, but this is not always the case in Japanese; the same word order as in the affirmative sentence may be used.

### 6. -sai

When referring to age, the counter suffix -**sai** is attached after the number which indicates the age. In asking a person's age, the interrogative **nan** is used as **nan-sai.** In asking a person's age more politely, **o-ikutsu** is used instead (**o**-indicates politeness). When replying to this type of question, -**sai** may be omitted.

(o-ikutsu)

| | |
|---|---|
| **Tanaka-san wa nan-sai desu ka.** | *How old are you, Mr. Tanaka?* |
| ··· **(Watashi wa) 28-sai desu.** | *···I am 28 years old.* |
| ···**28 desu.** | |

(See Lesson 11 and Appendix 1)

# Lesson 2

1. **Demonstrative words**

   1) **kore, sore** and **are**

      **kore** is used in referring to something that is close to the speaker.

      **sore** is used in referring to something close to the listener.

      **are** is used in referring to something remote from both the speaker and the listener.

      > **Kore wa hon desu.**          *This is a book.*

   2) **kono, sono** and **ano**

      **Kore, sore** and **are** do not precede a noun; **kono, sono** and **ano** are used instead to modify a noun.

      > **Kono hon wa watashi no desu.**          *This book is mine.*

2. **Hai, sō desu. Iie, sō dewa arimasen.**

   In answering to a question asked in a noun sentence, **sō** is often used as "**sō desu**", "**sō dewa arimasen**". Use of **sō** is convenient as it makes an answer brief and simple. Note, however, that "**sō desu**", or "**sō dewa arimasen**" cannot be used in answering a question asked in a sentence ending with a verb (see Lesson 4) or in a sentence ending with an adjective (see Lesson 8).

   > **Anata wa Tōkyō-kikai no kenshūsei desu ka.**
   >
   > *Are you a trainee of Tokyo Kikai Co., Ltd?*
   >
   > ⋯ **Hai, Tōkyō-kikai no kenshūsei desu.**
   >
   > ⋯ **Hai, sō desu.**          ⋯ *Yes, I am.*
   >
   > ⋯ **Iie, Tōkyō-kikai no kenshūsei dewa arimasen.**
   >
   > ⋯ **Iie, sō dewa arimasen.**          ⋯ *No, I am not.*

3. **Interrogative sentence** ... 2

   Alternative question: This is a type of interrogative sentence in which an answer is to be chosen out of alternatives ending with **ka.**

   > **Sore wa bōrupen desu ka, shāpupenshiru desu ka.**
   >
   > *Is it a ball-point pen, or a mechanical pencil?*
   >
   > ⋯**Bōrupen desu.**          ⋯ *It is a ball-point pen.*

   In answering this type of question, "**Hai**" or "**Iie**" is not used.

**4.** $\boxed{\text{N no N}}$ ... 2

1) This **no** indicates possession.

        **watashi no hon**   *my book*

2) The noun which is preceded by the possessive **no** is often omitted when the meaning is clear without it. However, when the noun is a person, it is not omitted.

    **Kore wa anata no tegami desu ka.**     *Is this your letter?*

    **···Hai, watashi no (tegami) desu.**     *···Yes, it is mine.*

    **Are wa dare no kaban desu ka.**     *Whose bag is that?*

    **···Kimura-san no (kaban) desu.**     *···It is Miss Kimura's.*

    **Anata wa Tōkyō-kikai no kenshūsei desu ka.**

        *Are you a trainee of Tokyo Kikai Co., Ltd?*

    **···Hai, Tōkyō-kikai no kenshūsei desu.**

        *···Yes, I am a trainee of Tokyo Kikai Co., Ltd.*

# Lesson 3

1 . koko, soko, asoko, doko, kochira, sochira, achira and dochira

The pronouns kore, sore and are that are discussed in Lesson 2 refer to a thing, while koko, soko, asoko and doko refer to a place. kochira, sochira, achira and dochira also refer to a place, but they are more polite expressions than koko, soko, asoko and doko.

2 . doko and dochira

The sentence below has two different meanings: (1) a question asking the name of the company, and (2) a question asking the location of the company. When dochira is used, the question is usually asking the name of the company.

Anata no kaisha wa {dochira / doko} desu ka.

*(1) What is the name of your company?*

*(2) Where is your company?*

3 . | N no N | ... 3

We have learned in Lesson 1 and Lesson 2 that no connects a noun with another noun and makes a possessive or indicates that one belongs to the other. There are other uses of no and the following are some examples for your reference.

| | |
|---|---|
| konpyūta no kaisha | *computer company* |
| Nihon no tokei | *Japanese watch* |
| kinō no ban | *last night* |

## 4. Demonstrative pronouns, adjectives

| demonstrative pronoun | demonstrative adjective | pronoun of place | pronoun indicating direction, side, place |
|---|---|---|---|
| kore *this* | kono *this* ┐ | koko *this place* | kochira *this direction, side, place* |
| sore *that* | sono *that* ├ +N | soko *that place* | sochira *that direction, side, place* |
| are *that over there* | ano *that over there* ┘ | asoko *that place over there* | achira *that direction, side, place over there* |
| dore *which* | dono *which* +N | doko *where* | dochira *where, which direction* |

## 5. ⬚ Sentence **ka** ... 2

Not all the sentences ending with the particle **ka** are interrogative. **ka** is also used at the end of a sentence when the speaker is trying to confirm what the other person has said.

**Kaban-uriba wa doko desu ka.**      *Where is the bag department?*

··· **Kaban-uriba desu <u>ka</u>. 5-kai desu.**

···*The bag department? It is on the 5th floor.*

10

# Lesson 4

### 1. -masu

-masu follows a verb to indicate the speaker's polite attitude.

| | |
|---|---|
| nemasu | *to sleep* |
| okimasu | *to get up* |
| hatarakimasu | *to work* |

### 2. Inflection of -masu

In Japanese a verb takes two forms: one denotes the past time reference and perfective aspect, and the other denotes the present and future tenses or a habit or fact which has no temporal reference. -masu inflects as shown below.

| | non-past | past |
|---|---|---|
| affirmative | (oki)-masu | (oki)-mashita |
| negative | (oki)-masen | (oki)-masendeshita |

| | |
|---|---|
| Maiasa 6-ji ni okimasu. | *I get up at 6 o'clock every morning.* |
| Ashita 6-ji ni okimasu. | *I will get up at 6 o'clock tomorrow.* |
| Kinō 6-ji ni okimashita. | *I got up at 6 o'clock yesterday.* |

### 3. -ji and -fun (-pun)

To express time, a counter suffix is put after the number (See Appendices 2, ENGLISH TRANSLATION, SHIN NIHONGO NO KISO I.)

| -ji | *o'clock* | | | | |
|---|---|---|---|---|---|
| | | ichi-ji | *one o'clock* | | |
| | | ni-ji | *two* | *〃* | |
| | | san-ji | *three* | *〃* | |
| | | yo-ji | *four* | *〃* | (not shi-ji or yon-ji) |
| | | go-ji | *five* | *〃* | |
| | | roku-ji | *six* | *〃* | |
| | | shichi-ji | *seven* | *〃* | (not nana-ji) |
| | | hachi-ji | *eight* | *〃* | |
| | | ku-ji | *nine* | *〃* | (not kyū-ji) |
| | | jū-ji | *ten* | *〃* | |
| | | jū ichi-ji | *eleven* | *〃* | |
| | | jū ni-ji | *twelve* | *〃* | |
| | | nan-ji | *what time?* | | |

| | | | |
|---|---|---|---|
| -fun | *minute(s)* | ip-pun | *one minute* |
| | | ni-fun | *two minutes* |
| | | san-pun | *"* |
| | | yon-pun | *four "* (not **shi-fun** or **yo-fun**) |
| | | go-fun | *five "* |
| | | rop-pun | *six "* |
| | | { nana-fun<br>{ shichi-fun | *seven "* |
| | | hap-pun | *eight "* |
| | | kyū-fun | *nine "* (not **ku-fun**) |
| | | { jup-pun<br>{ jip-pun | *ten "* |
| | | nan-pun | *how many minutes?* |

＊ **-fun** is pronounced as **-pun** when preceded by some numerals.

**4 . Particle ni ... 1**

| N (time) **ni** | *at ....* |

The point in time when the action takes place is indicated by putting the particle **ni** after the noun which denotes the time, but only when time is expressed using numerals.

**Watashi wa 6-ji ni okimasu.**      *I get up at 6 o'clock.*

**9-gatsu 15-nichi ni Nihon e kimashita.**

     *I came to Japan on September 15th.*     (See Lesson 5)

**Kinō ni̶ benkyō-shimashita.**      *I studied yesterday.*

**Konban ni̶ benkyō-shimasu.**      *I will study tonight.*

**ni** may be used with the days of the week, but it is not essential.

**Nichi-yōbi (ni) Tōkyō e ikimasu.**

     *I am going to Tokyo on Sunday.*     (See Lesson 5)

**5 . Particles kara and made**

| N (time/place) **kara** N (time/place) **made** |

1 ) **kara** indicates the starting time/place, while **made** indicates the end or destination of time/place.

**9-ji kara 5-ji made hatarakimasu.**

     *I work from 9 o'clock to 5 o'clock.*

**Tōkyō kara Ōsaka made donokurai kakarimasu ka.**

     *How long does it take from Tokyo to Osaka?* (See Lesson 11)

2 ) ～**kara** and ～**made** are not always used together in a sentence.

**9-ji kara Nihon-go o benkyō-shimasu.**

     *I study Japanese from 9 o'clock.*

**12-ji made Nihon-go o benkyō-shimasu.**

*I study Japanese until 12 o'clock.*

3) **kara** or **made** is not always followed by a verb.

**Nihon-go no benkyō wa 9-ji kara desu.**

*Japanese language study is from 9 o'clock.*

① **benkyō-shimasu** is a verb and is constructed by connecting the noun **benkyō** to the verb **shimasu**. "**Nihon-go no benkyō**", therefore, means *study of Japanese language.*

② The particle **ni** always precedes a verb; unlike **kara** or **made**, it is never followed by **desu.**

**6-ji ni okimasu.**      *I get up at 6 o'clock.*

**Ima 8-ji ꜜ desu.**      *It is 8 o'clock now.*

## 6. Sō desu ka

This is uttered with a falling intonation to lightly show agreement or to express exclamation or a sense of being impressed.

A: **Nihon-go no benkyō wa nan-ji made desu ka.**

*Until what time do you study Japanese?*

B: **12-ji made desu.**      *Up to 12 o'clock.*

A: **Sō desu ka.**↘      *Is that so?*

## 7. [ Sentence   ne ] ... 1

**ne** is put at the end of a sentence to add feeling or to seek agreement from the listener. (**ne** is not used in a monologue. )

**Benkyō wa 9-ji kara 5-ji made desu.**

*I study from 9 o'clock to 5 o'clock.*

··· **Sore wa taihen desu ne.**      ···*That's very hard, isn't it.*

**Ii shatsu desu ne.**

*That's a nice shirt, isn't it?* (See Lesson 7)

··· **Kore desu ka. Tomodachi ni moraimashita.**

··· *This shirt? My friend gave me this.*

13

# Lesson 5

## 1. Particle e

When a verb indicating a move to a certain place, such as **ikimasu**, **kimasu**, **kaerimasu**, etc., is used in the predicate, the particle **e** is put after the place noun to show the direction of the move.

**Kyōto e ikimasu.**    *I will go to Kyoto.*

## 2. ☐ Interrogative + (particle) + **mo** + negative ☐

doko (e)
nani    ⎱ **mo ~ -masen** (negative).    *I do not....*  ⎱ *anywhere....*
dare                                                      *anything....*
                                                          *anybody....*

When **mo** comes immediately after an interrogative in a negative sentence, all that belongs to the category represented by the interrogative is denied.

**Doko (e) mo ikimasen.**    *(I) don't go anywhere.*

**Nani mo tabemasen.**    *(I) do not eat anything.* (See Lesson 6)

**Dare mo imasen.**    *Nobody is there.*    (See Lesson 10)

## 3. Particle de ... 1

☐ N(vehicle)  **de** ☐    *by (vehicle)*

The particle **de** indicates a means or a method used. When verbs denoting a move (**ikimasu**, **kimasu**, etc.) are used with **de**, **de** indicates a means of transportation. A noun preceding **de** indicates the kind of transportation.

**Densha de ikimasu.**    *(I) will go by train.*

## 4. Particle to ... 1

☐ N(person)  **to** ☐    *with (person)*

The particle **to** that follows a noun denoting a person means *together with* ~ or *accompanied by* ~.

**Tomodachi to Nihon e kimashita.**

*I came to Japan with my friend.*

**5.** Sentence **yo**

**yo** is a particle used at the end of a sentence to emphasize information that the listener does not know or to show one is giving one's judgement or views strongly. **yo** pronounced with a stress would sound pushy, so it should be pronounced lightly as if simply adding a sound at the end of the sentence.

**Kono densha wa Yokohama e ikimasu ka.**

*Is this train going to Yokohama?*

**···Iie, ikimasen. 3-bansen desu yo.**

*··· No, it's not. That's on platform 3.*

**Kono mise wa hanbāgu ga oishii desu yo.**

*The hamburger steaks in this restaurant are very good!*

(See Lesson 16)

# Lesson 6

**1. Particle o ... 1**

> N   o   V (transitive)

The particle **o** indicates the object of a verb.  Unlike English, the word order in Japanese is Subject - Object - Verb.

> **Kōhii o nomimasu.**     *(I) drink coffee.*
>
> **Shatsu o kaimasu.**     *(I) will buy a shirt.*

**2. Particle de ... 2**

> N (place)   **de**

The **de** discussed here comes after a noun denoting a place and indicates the place where the action occurs.

> **Kyōshitsu de Nihon-go o benkyō-shimasu.**
>
> *(I) study Japanese in the classroom.*

**3. Particle to ... 2**

> N   **to**   N

**to** connects a noun with another noun in coordinate relation.

> **Pan to tamago o tabemasu.**     *(I) eat bread and eggs.*

**4. Nan and Nani**

Both **nan** and **nani** mean *what*, but in the following cases **nan** is used.

1) When it precedes a word starting with **d**, **t** or **n**.

> **Nan desu ka.**     *What is it?*
>
> **Nan no kaisha desu ka.**     *What company is it?*
>
> **Nan to iimashita ka.**     *What did (he) say?*     (See Lesson 21)

2) When followed by a counter suffix or the like.

> **nan-sai**     *how old?*
>
> **nan-ban**     *what number?*
>
> **nan-yōbi**     *what day of the week?*

**nani** is used in all other cases.

> **Nani o nomimasu ka.**     *What would you like to drink?*

## 5. V-masen ka

This expression is not a real question, but an invitation to the listener to do something.

**Issho ni gohan o tabemasen ka.** *Won't you have lunch with me?*

## 6. V-mashō

This expression is used when the speaker is positively inviting the listener to do something with him. It is also used when responding positively to such an invitation.

**Robii de yasumimashō.** *Let's take a rest in the lobby.*

**Issho ni depāto e ikimasen ka.**

*Won't you go to the department store with me?*

**···Ē, ikimashō.** *··· Yes, let's go.*

# Lesson 7

**1. Particle de . . . 3**

| N (tool/means) de |   *with...., in...., by....*

We learned **de** that indicates a means of transportation in Lesson 5, and **de** that indicates a place in Lesson 6. Here we will learn **de** that indicates a means or method used for an action.

        **Hashi de gohan o tabemasu.**      *(I) eat rice with chopsticks.*

        **Nihon-go de repōto o kakimasu.**      *(I) write a report in Japanese.*

**2. Particle ni . . . 2**

1)

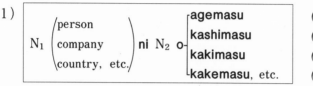

    *(I) will give $N_2$ to $N_1$.*
    *(I) will lend $N_2$ to $N_1$.*
    *(I) will write $N_2$ on $N_1$.*
    *(I) will make a phone call ($N_2$) to $N_1$, etc.*

**ni** in this sense is used together with a verb which denotes giving a thing, etc., such as **agemasu** *to give* and **denwa o kakemasu** *to make a phone call*, and indicates the indirect object of the action.

        **Watashi wa Narong-san ni tokei o agemasu.**

           *I will give a watch to Mr. Narong.*

        **Kaisha ni denwa o kakemasu.**

           *I will make a phone call to the company.*

2)

$$N_1 \begin{pmatrix} \text{person} \\ \text{company} \\ \text{country, etc.} \end{pmatrix} \begin{Bmatrix} \text{ni} \\ \text{kara} \end{Bmatrix} N_2 \text{ o} \begin{Bmatrix} \text{naraimasu} \\ \text{moraimasu, etc.} \end{Bmatrix}$$

    *(I) learn $N_2$ from $N_1$.*
    *(I) receive $N_2$ from $N_1$.*
    *etc.*

**ni** in the above pattern used together with a verb which denotes receiving a thing or information, such as **moraimasu** *to receive* and **naraimasu** *to learn*, etc., indicates the source of the thing or information. **ni** in this pattern may be replaced by **kara** in most instances. When $N_1$ is not a person but an organization such as a company or a school, **kara** is usually used instead.

Watashi wa tomodachi $\begin{Bmatrix} \text{ni} \\ \text{kara} \end{Bmatrix}$ tokei o moraimashita.

*I received a watch from my friend.*

**Watashi wa kaisha kara tokei o moraimashita.**

*I received a watch from the company.*

3. **mō** and **mada**

The adverb **mō** means *already* and the adverb **mada** means *yet*.

**Mō hiru-gohan o tabemashita ka.**      *Have you already had lunch?*

··· **Hai, mō tabemashita.**

··· *Yes, I have already had lunch.*

··· **Iie, mada desu.**      ··· *No, not yet.*

×··· **Iie, mada tabemasendeshita.**
                                    *

\* **mada** means *yet* or *up until then* or *now* and indicates that a certain action or state has not occurred or has not yet been completed by the time of speaking. Therefore, a verb which denotes the fact in the past tense, i.e. **-masendeshita**, cannot occur with **mada**.

4. **Hai and Iie**

As we saw in Lesson 1, **Hai** and **Iie** are used in answering a question which does not include an interrogative nor an alternative question. In Japanese when one agrees to the content of a question, **Hai** is used in response, while **Iie** is used when one does not agree to the content of the question. Use of **Hai** or **Iie** is not determined by whether the sentence preceded by **Hai** or **Iie** is an affirmative or a negative sentence.

In response to the negative question **Ikimasen ka** *"Aren't you going?"*, the listener will answer **Iie, ikimasu**, *"No, I am going"*, meaning *"What you have said is not correct. I am going"*. If the listener is not going, he or she will say **Hai, ikimasen**, *"Yes, I am not going,"* meaning *"What you have said is right. I am not going"*.

**Ikimasen ka.**      *Aren't you going?*

··· **Iie, ikimasu.**      ··· *No. I am going.*

··· **Hai, ikimasen.**      ··· *Yes. I am not going.*

1) **Hai** and **Ē**

**Hai** is used in a formal context, while in informal situations **Ē** is often used instead.

2) **Hai** and **Ē** also are used frequently for light chiming-in during conversation.

# Lesson 8

**Adjectives**

**1 . Adjectives as modifiers**

In Japanese an adjective which modifies a noun is put before the noun. There are two types of adjectives:

　　a ) i-adjective [A]

　　b ) na-adjective [Na]

When modifying a noun, those adjectives ending with i are called i-adjectives [A] and those with na are called na-adjectives [Na].

　　　　**Tōkyō wa ōkii machi desu.**　　　*Tokyo is a big city.*

　　　　**Rao-san wa shinsetsuna hito desu.**　*Mr. Rao is a kind person.*

1 ) All i-adjectives end with -i. (The sound preceding -i is either a, i, u or o. )

| chiisai | *small* | ōkii | *big* |
|---------|---------|------|-------|
| atsui | *hot* | omoi | *heavy* |

2 ) na-adjectives end either with any sound other than -i or -ei; kirai is an exception (See Lesson 9).

| shinsetsu | *kind* | kirei | *beautiful* |
|-----------|--------|-------|-------------|
| shizuka | *quiet* | yūmei | *famous* |

**2. Adjectives that function as predicates**

1 ) Non-past affirmative

When an adjective is used as a non-past affirmative predicate, i-adjectives remain unchanged, but the -na of na-adjectives is omitted.

　　　　**Tōkyō wa ōkii desu.**　　　*Tokyo is big.*

　　　　**Rao-san wa shinsetsu desu.**　*Mr. Rao is kind.*

2 ) Non-past negative

　　① Negative form of i-adjectives

　　　　**atsui desu.**　　　　　　　*It is hot.*
　　　　　　↓
　　　　**atsukunai desu.**　　　　　*It is not hot.*

　　　　**Tai wa ima atsukunai desu.**　*It is not hot in Thailand now.*

Exception: The negative form of ii desu is yokunai desu.

　　　　**Kono jisho wa ii desu.** (affirmative)　*This dictionary is good.*

　　　　**Kono jisho wa yokunai desu.** (negative)　*This dictionary is not good.*

② Negative form of **na**-adjectives

shizuka <u>desu.</u>　　　　　　　　　*It is quiet.*
 ↓
shizuka <u>dewa arimasen.</u>　　　　*It is not quiet.*
Tōkyō wa shizuka dewa arimasen.　*Tokyo is not quiet.*

|  | non-past | |
|---|---|---|
|  | i-adjective | na-adjective |
| affirmative | takai desu | shizuka desu |
| negative | takakunai desu | shizuka dewa arimasen |

### 3. amari ～ -masen (negative)

**amari** *so much* is an adverb and is used in a negative sentence with a verb or an adjective that functions as a predicate. It means that the degree of the action or the state is not very intense or significant.

 **Tai wa ima amari atsukunai desu.**
  *It is not so hot in Thailand now.*
 **Nihon wa amari shizuka dewa arimasen.**
  *Japan is not very quiet.*
 **O-sake o amari nomimasen.**　　　*I don't drink alcohol so much.*

### 4. (～wa) dō desu ka　*How do you like ....*

**dō** is an interrogative word used to ask an impression or the state of a person or a thing.

 **Nihon no tabemono wa dō desu ka.**　*How do you like Japanese food?*
 ··· **Oishii desu ga, takai desu.**　　　*··· It is good, but expensive.*

### 5. donna + N ... 1　*What kind of ....*

**donna** is an interrogative word used to ask the characteristics or the nature or intrinsic condition of a thing(s) or a person(s) and is put in front of the noun.

 **Kimura-san wa donna hito desu ka.**
  *What kind of a person is Miss Kimura?*
 ··· **Kireina hito desu.**　　　　　*··· She is beautiful.*

### 6. ～ga, ～　*....., but ....*

**ga** is used as a conjunction to connect a sentence with another sentence when what is to be stated in the latter is contrary to what is expected from the former.

 **Nihon no tabemono wa oishii desu ga, takai desu.**
  *Japanese food is good, but expensive.*

7. **Soshite**   *And*

While **to** (as we have already learned in Lesson 6) is used to connect a noun with another noun, **soshite** is used to connect sentences.

> **Kimura-san wa kireina hito desu. Soshite taihen shinsetsu desu.**
> *Miss Kimura is a beautiful person. And she is very kind.*

8. **dore**   *which*

This is an interrogative word used to specify one from among three or more things specifically presented.

> **Rao-san no kaban wa dore desu ka.**     *Which is Mr. Rao's bag?*
> ⋯ **Ano kuroi kaban desu.**     *⋯ That black bag is.*

# Lesson 9

1.

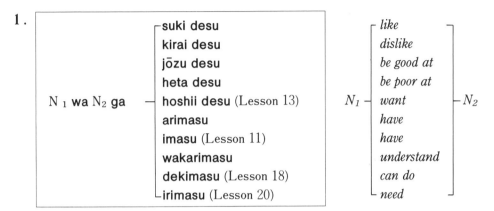

We have learned sentences in which the object of a verb action is denoted by the particle **o**. Here we will learn sentences in which the object of a predicate is indicated by **ga**. These sentences have predicates that mean the following:

1) Predicates that refer to the speaker's frame of mind such as preference or desire.

   **suki desu, kirai desu, hoshii desu,** etc.

2) Those which refer to one's ability.

   **jōzu desu, heta desu, wakarimasu,** etc.

3) Those which refer to possession.

   **arimasu, imasu**

The above predicates mark the object not with **o** but with **ga**.

   **Watashi wa ringo ga suki desu.**     *I like apples.*

   **Lee-san wa kanji ga wakarimasu.**

   *Mr. Lee understands kanji.*

The above mentioned words may be grouped according to the parts of speech as follows:

   **suki, kirai, jōzu, heta**           ---- **na**-adjectives

   **hoshii**                            ---- **i**-adjective

   **wakarimasu, arimasu, imasu, dekimasu, irimasu**

                                         ---- verbs (that denote states)

## 2. donna + N ... 2

In addition to the usage which we learned in Lesson 8, "**donna**+N" may be asked to pick up one specific thing out of a group of things.

**Donna supōtsu ga suki desu ka.**

*What kind of sports do you like?*

··· **Tenisu ga suki desu.**      ··· *I like tennis.*

## 3. zenzen ~ masen (negative)

**zenzen** is used in a negative sentence in which the predicate is either an adjective or a verb to deny totally what is described by the adjective or the verb.

**Kanji ga zenzen wakarimasen.**      *I don't understand kanji at all.*

## 4. dōshite      *Why*

This is an interrogative for asking a reason.

A : **Kinō kaisha o yasumimashita.**

*I took a day off from the company yesterday.*

B : **Dōshite yasumimashita ka.**      *Why did you take a day off?*

A : **Netsu ga arimashita kara.**      *Because I had a fever.*

## 5. | Sentence/Phrase kara |  *Because ....*

**kara** is attached at the end of a sentence or a phrase to state a reason(s).

**Onaka ga itai desu kara, nani mo tabemasen.**

*As I have a stomachache, I won't eat anything.*

∗ Note that the position of **kara** in a sentence is different from that of its English equivalent.

# Lesson 10

## 1. arimasu, imasu

These verbs denote the presence of a thing(s) or a person(s).

1) When what is present is inanimate, or does not move by itself, although it is animate, **arimasu** is used.

| | | | |
|---|---|---|---|
| **terebi** | *television(set)* | **tsukue** | *desk* |
| **tabako** | *cigarette* | **hana** | *flower, etc.* |

2) When what is present is animate and moves by itself, such as people or animals, **imasu** is used.

| | | | |
|---|---|---|---|
| **Tanaka-san** | *Mr. Tanaka* | **kenshūsei** | *trainee* |
| **inu** | *dog, etc.* | | |

① **Terebi ga arimasu.**  *There is a television.*

② **Tanaka-san ga imasu.**  *There is Mr. Tanaka.*

## 2. Particle ni ... 3

> N (place)  **ni**

The place where a thing or a person is present is indicated by the particle **ni**.

**Robii <u>ni</u> terebi ga arimasu.**  *There is a television in the lobby.*

**Jimusho <u>ni</u> Tanaka-san ga imasu.**  *Mr. Tanaka is in the office.*

## 3.

> N₂ **ni** N₁ **ga** { arimasu / imasu }  *There is(are) $N_1$ at/on/in $N_2$*

This is a sentence which describes the fact, such as a scene, as it is. The subject of such a sentence is marked with the particle **ga**.

**Robii ni terebi <u>ga</u> arimasu.**  *There is a television in the lobby.*

**Jimusho ni Tanaka-san <u>ga</u> imasu.**  *Mr. Tanaka is in the office.*

## 4.

> N₁ **wa** N₂ **ni** { arimasu / imasu }  *$N_1$ is at/on/in $N_2$.*

This sentence refers to the whereabouts of a thing(s) or a person(s).

**Hon wa tsukue no ue ni arimasu.**  *The book is on the desk.*

**Rao-san wa heya ni imasu.**  *Mr. Rao is in the room.*

Therefore when the whereabouts of a thing which is understood by both the speaker and the listener is asked, the following sentence pattern is used.

$\boxed{\text{N}_1 \text{ (understood object)}}$ **wa doko ni arimasu ka.**  *Where is N₁?*

On the other hand, when the question refers to a thing in connection with the description of a scene or fact, the following sentence pattern is used.

$\boxed{\text{N}_2}$ **ni nani ga arimasu ka.**  *What is there/at/on/in N₂?*

5.

The sentence "N₁ **wa** N₂ **ni arimasu/imasu**" may be replaced by "N₁ **wa** N₂ **desu**".

**Hon wa tsukue no ue <u>ni arimasu</u>.**  *The book is on the desk.*

↓

**desu**

**Rao-san wa heya <u>ni imasu</u>.**  *Mr. Rao is in the room.*

↓

**desu**

＊Note that the particle **ni** is not used after a noun which denotes a place (**tsukue no ue, heya**) when **desu** is used.

6. **Particle ya**

$\boxed{\text{N } \textbf{ya} \text{ N}}$

The particle **to** (which we learned in Lesson 6) is used when enumerating all the items, while the particle **ya**, which we will learn here, is used for referring to two or three representative items out of many.

**Tsukue no ue ni hon to pen ga arimasu.**

*There are some books and pens on the desk.*

**Tsukue no ue ni hon ya pen ga arimasu.**

*There are some books and pens, etc., on the desk.*

# Lesson 11

## 1. Counting numbers

### 1) hitotsu, futatsu,......tō

This usage is employed in counting numbers. In counting 11 and above, simple numbers are used without **-tsu**.

### 2) **Counter suffix**

When counting things or expressing the quantity of things, counter suffixes are attached after numbers. Different suffixes are used depending on the things to be counted.

-nin     number of people

         3：san-nin     4：yo-nin

         However, one person is **hitori** and two persons, **futari**. For three or more, **nin** is attached.

-dai        machines and vehicles (such as typewriters, cars, etc.)

         1：ichi-dai    2：ni-dai

-mai       thin and flat things (such as paper, dishes, etc.)

         1：ichi-mai    2：ni-mai

-en         amount of money (See Lesson 3)

         1：ichi-en     2：ni-en

-kai/do    times

         1：ik-kai      2：ni-kai

         ichi-do         ni-do

-ban       order in a series (See Lesson 16)

         1：ichi-ban    2：ni-ban

-kai        floors (See Lesson 3)

         1：ik-kai      2：ni-kai         3：san-gai

-fun/pun   minutes

         1：ip-pun     2：ni-fun

-jikan      hours

         1：ichi-jikan   2：ni-jikan

-nichi      days

         1：ichi-nichi   15：jū go-nichi

-shūkan    weeks

         1：is-shūkan   2：ni-shūkan

-kagetsu  months

      1 : ik-kagetsu  2 : ni-kagetsu

-nen     years

      1 : ichi-nen    2 : ni-nen

-sai     age

      1 : is-sai     2 : ni-sai

(See Appendices, ENGLISH TRANSLATION, **SHIN NIHONGO NO KISO I**)

3 ) **Usage of quantifiers**

Here we will mainly learn the usage of quantifiers that function as adverbs modifying a verb.

     **Ringo o hitotsu tabemashita.**     *I ate one apple.*

     **Kyōdai ga 3-nin imasu.**     *I have three brothers.*

## 2 . Interrogative quantifiers

The interrogative form of asking numbers is "**nan** + counter suffix", such as **nan-nin, nan-dai** and **nan-mai**, etc.

     **Jidōsha ga nan-dai arimasu ka.**     *How many cars are there?*

The interrogative form of **hitotsu** and **futatsu**, however, is **ikutsu**.

     **Kyōshitsu ni tsukue ga ikutsu arimasu ka.**

       *How many desks are there in the classroom?*

     ··· **12 arimasu.**       ··· *There are 12.*

When it is necessary to specify the unit of currency, **nan-en** is used as an interrogative; otherwise, **ikura** is generally used.

## 3 . N, etc. dake

**dake** is attached after a noun or a noun equivalent and it specifies the quantity, scope or extent of what is denoted by the noun.

     **Kuni de 3-shūkan dake Nihon-go o benkyō-shimashita.**

     *I studied Japanese for only three weeks in my country.*

## 4 . donokurai (or donogurai)

**donokurai** is widely used to ask the amount of money, length, distance, quantity or number. The meaning varies depending on the predicate which follows it.

In this lesson we will learn ways of asking lengths of time. **nan**+counter suffix can be used in place of **donokurai**.

     **Tōkyō kara Kyōto made donokurai kakarimasu ka.**

     *How long does it take to go from Tokyo to Kyoto?*

     **Tōkyō kara Kyōto made nan-jikan kakarimasu ka.**

     *How many hours does it take to go from Tokyo to Kyoto?*

# Lesson 12

1. Tense/affirmative/negative of desu in noun sentences and na-adjective sentences.

|  | non-past (present, future) | past |
|---|---|---|
| affirmative | ame (N)<br>shizuka (Na) } desu | ame<br>shizuka } deshita |
| negative | ame<br>shizuka } dewa arimasen | ame<br>shizuka } dewa arimasen<br>deshita |

Non-past forms of desu are used both for the present and future tenses, as are non-past forms of -masu.

| | |
|---|---|
| Kyō wa getsu-yōbi desu. | *Today is Monday.* |
| Ashita wa ka-yōbi desu. | *Tomorrow is Tuesday.* |
| Kyō wa hima desu. | *I am free today.* |
| Ashita wa hima desu. | *I am free tomorrow.* |
| Kinō wa ame deshita ka. | *Did it rain yesterday?* |
| ··· Hai, ame deshita. | *··· Yes, it did.* |
| ··· Iie, ame dewa arimasendeshita. | *··· No, it didn't.* |

2. Tense/affirmative/negative of i-adjectives

|  | non-past | past |
|---|---|---|
| affirmative | atsui desu | atsukatta desu |
| negative | atsukunai desu | atsukunakatta desu |

| | |
|---|---|
| Kinō wa atsukatta desu ka. | *Was it hot yesterday?* |
| ··· Hai, atsukatta desu. | *··· Yes, it was.* |
| ··· Iie, atsukunakatta desu. | *··· No, it wasn't.* |

3. Comparison

Unlike English adjectives, adjectives in Japanese do not have comparative and superlative forms; meanings of the comparative or the superlative are expressed by placing a particle or an adverb in front of the adjective.

1 ) Comparison between two

a)

$$\boxed{\text{N}_1 \text{ wa N}_2 \text{ yori } \begin{Bmatrix} \text{A} \\ \text{Na} \end{Bmatrix} \text{ desu}}$$   *$N_1$ is more $\begin{Bmatrix} A \\ Na \end{Bmatrix}$ than $N_2$.*

Comparison is made with $N_2$ as a benchmark to describe the quality and/or state of $N_1$.

**Tōkyō wa Ōsaka yori ōkii desu.**   *Tokyo is bigger than Osaka.*

b) Questions and answers of comparison between two items

① Question

$$\boxed{\text{N}_1 \text{ to N}_2 \text{ to, dochira ga } \begin{Bmatrix} \text{A} \\ \text{Na} \end{Bmatrix} \text{ desu ka}}$$   *Which is more $\begin{Bmatrix} A \\ Na \end{Bmatrix}$ $N_1$ or $N_2$?*

**Shinkansen to hikōki to, dochira ga hayai desu ka.**

*Which is faster, Shinkansen or airplane?*

**Niku to sakana to, dochira ga suki desu ka.**

*Which do you like better, meat or fish?*

When comparing two items, the interrogative **dochira** is always used for people, things, places or time.

② Answer

$$\boxed{\text{N}_1/\text{N}_2 \text{ no hō ga } \begin{Bmatrix} \text{A} \\ \text{Na} \end{Bmatrix} \text{ desu}}$$   *$N_1/N_2$ is more $\begin{Bmatrix} A \\ Na \end{Bmatrix}$*

**Hikōki no hō ga hayai desu.**   *Airplane is faster.*

**Sakana no hō ga suki desu.**   *I like fish better.*

2 ) In choosing one out of an entire family, order, set, group, category

$$\boxed{\text{N (no naka) de} \begin{bmatrix} \text{nani} \\ \text{doko} \\ \text{dare} \\ \text{itsu} \end{bmatrix} \text{ga ichiban } \begin{Bmatrix} \text{A} \\ \text{Na} \end{Bmatrix} \text{ desu ka}}$$   *$\begin{bmatrix} Which \\ Where \\ Who \\ When \end{bmatrix}$ is the most $\begin{Bmatrix} A \\ Na \end{Bmatrix}$ among N?*

**Supōtsu (no naka) de, <u>nani</u> ga ichiban suki desu ka.**
        \*

*What do you like best among the sports?*

··· **Sakkā ga ichiban suki desu.**   *··· I like soccer best.*

**Kurasu de <u>dare</u> ga ichiban wakai desu ka.**
        \*

*Who is the youngest in the class?*

··· **Narong-san ga ichiban wakai desu.**   *··· Mr. Narong is the youngest.*

\* The interrogative word used varies according to the group out of which selection is made.

30

# Lesson 13

1. | (Watashi wa)  N  ga hoshii desu |     *(I) want N.*

As we have seen in Lesson 9, words which become the object of a predicate denoting a frame of mind, such as preference and desire, are marked by **ga**. **hoshii** is an **i**-adjective.

> Watashi wa kamera ga hoshii desu.     *I want a camera.*
> Watashi wa kamera ga hoshikunai desu.     *I don't want a camera.*

2. | (Watashi wa)  N  o  V-tai desu |     *(I) want to (infinitive).*

The form made of V-**masu** (**tabemasu**) less -**masu** (**tabe**) is called **masu**-form. (See p.104, **Renshū A, Dai 13 ka, SHIN NIHONGO NO KISO I**) Only a noun can be the object of **hoshii** in the above. When you want to do some action, this expression is used.

> nomimasu  →  nomitai desu
> tabemasu  →  tabetai desu, etc.

Tense, affirmative and negative forms of V-**tai** are constructed in the same way as those of **i**-adjectives.

|  | non-past | past |
|---|---|---|
| affirmative | nomitai desu | nomitakatta desu |
| negative | nomitakunai desu | nomitakunakatta desu |

The object of a verb denoting an action is marked by **o**. In this expression, if the attention is placed on the action, **o** may be attached after N to make it an object, while if the attention is placed on the speaker's frame of mind, as indicated by -**tai**, **ga** may be attached after N to make it an object of the predicate **nomitai**. In this expression, therefore, either **o** or **ga** may be used after N.

> Biiru {o / ga} nomitai desu.     *I want to drink beer.*

In general, however, particles denoting the object of a transitive verb other than **o** cannot be replaced by **ga**.

> Kyōto e ikitai desu.     *I want to go to Kyoto.*
>        ~~ga~~
> 8-ji ni Sentā o detai desu.     *I want to leave the Center at 8 o'clock.*
>            ~~ga~~

∗ Note that **hoshii** and **-tai** are expressions for stating the desire of the speaker and, therefore, you might sound impolite to the listener if you ask a question such as **hoshii desu ka** or **-tai desu ka.**

3.

$$
\text{masu-form} + \text{ni} -
\begin{bmatrix}
\text{ikimasu} \\
\text{kimasu} \\
\text{kaerimasu}
\end{bmatrix}
\qquad (I) \quad
\begin{bmatrix}
\text{go} \\
\text{come} \\
\text{return}
\end{bmatrix}
\begin{cases}
\text{for} \\
\text{in order to}
\end{cases}
$$

The destination of movement for **ikimasu, kimasu** and **kaerimasu** that we learned in Lesson 5 is indicated by **e**; the purpose of the action is indicated by the **masu**-form + **ni.**

| | |
|---|---|
| Depāto e ikimasu. | *I (will) go to the department store.* |
| Kutsu o kaimasu. | *I (will) buy shoes.* |

→**Depāto e kutsu o kai ni ikimasu.**

*I (will) go to the department store to buy shoes.*

When a verb is derived from a noun denoting an action, however, the following expression may also be used.

| | |
|---|---|
| Nihon e kimashita. | *I came to Japan.* |
| Jidōsha o jisshū-shimasu. | *I (will) have practical training on cars.* |

→**Nihon e jidōsha o jisshū-shi ni kimashita.**

*I have come to Japan to have practical training on cars.*

∗→**Nihon e jidōsha no jisshū ni kimashita.**

*I have come to Japan for practical training on cars.*

∗ As **jisshū** in this sentence is a noun denoting an action, **o** may be replaced by **no.** In this way a noun may be used in place of the **masu**-form of a verb in this sentence pattern.

Nouns denoting an action can be transformed into verbs by adding **shimasu** as shown below:

| | | |
|---|---|---|
| sanpo | → | sanpo-shimasu |
| jisshū | → | jisshū-shimasu |
| benkyō | → | benkyō-shimasu |

4. **Particle ni**...4, **Particle o**...2

When the particle **ni** is used together with **hairimasu, norimasu** (Lesson 16), etc., it indicates one's destination. When the particle **o** is also used together with **demasu,** or **orimasu** (Lesson 16), it indicates a starting point or place.

| | |
|---|---|
| Heya ni hairimasu. | *I (will) enter the room.* |
| Densha ni norimasu. | *I (will) take a train.* |
| Heya o demasu. | *I (will) leave the room.* |
| Densha o orimasu. | *I (will) get off the train.* |

# Lesson 14

1. **Groups of verbs**

   Verbs in Japanese change their forms, i.e., they conjugate, and they are divided into three groups according to the types of conjugation.

   1) **Group I verbs**

      In the verbs of this group the syllable preceding -**masu** ends with the **i** line.

      | | |
      |---|---|
      | kakimasu | *write* |
      | nomimasu | *drink* |

   2) **Group II verbs**

      In most of the verbs of this group, the syllable preceding -**masu** ends with [-e], but some verbs have the syllable ending with [-i] which precedes -**masu**.

      | | |
      |---|---|
      | tabemasu | *eat* |
      | misemasu | *show* |
      | mimasu | *see* |

   3) **Group III verbs**

      Verbs of this group include **shimasu** and "noun denoting an action + **shimasu**", which we saw in Lesson 13, as well as **kimasu**.

      | | |
      |---|---|
      | shimasu | *do* |
      | benkyō-shimasu | *study* |
      | jisshū-shimasu | *have practical training* |
      | kimasu | *come* |

2. **How to construct the te-form** (See p.114, Renshū A, Dai 14 ka, SHIN NIHON-GO NO KISO I)

   Group II

   | | | | |
   |---|---|---|---|
   | tabe-masu | → | tabe-te | *eat* |
   | oshie-masu | → | oshie-te | *teach* |
   | mi-masu | → | mi-te | *see* |
   | oki-masu | → | oki-te | *get up* |

   Group III

   | | | | |
   |---|---|---|---|
   | ki-masu | → | ki-te | *come* |
   | shi-masu | → | shi-te | *do* |

   Group I

   | | | | |
   |---|---|---|---|
   | kaki-masu | → | kai-te | *write* |
   | kiki-masu | → | kii-te | *listen* |

| | | | |
|---|---|---|---|
| *iki-masu | → | it-te | *go* (* exception) |
| isogi-masu | → | isoi-de | *hurry* |
| nomi-masu | → | non-de | *drink* |
| yomi-masu | → | yon-de | *read* |
| yobi-masu | → | yon-de | *call* |
| furi-masu | → | fut-te | *fall* |
| kaeri-masu | → | kaet-te | *return* |
| ari-masu | → | at-te | *have, exist* |
| machi-masu | → | mat-te | *wait* |
| tachi-masu | → | tat-te | *stand* |
| kai-masu | → | kat-te | *buy* |
| sui-masu | → | sut-te | *smoke* |
| ii-masu | → | it-te | *say* |
| hanashi-masu | → | hanashi-te | *speak* |
| kashi-masu | → | kashi-te | *lend* |

**3. Following phrases and the te-form**

In Japanese various phrases are connected to the end of conjugated verbs to construct sentences of various meanings. The following are some of the sentence patterns using the **te**-form.

**4. Use of the te-form ... 1—A**

| V-te kudasai |  *Please do....for me.*

This sentence pattern is used to ask or encourage the listener to do something. In this lesson we will learn expressions for making requests.

| Chotto matte kudasai. | *Please wait a moment.* |
| Jisho o kashite kudasai. | *Please lend me the dictionary.* |
| Yukkuri hanashite kudasai. | *Please speak slowly.* |

**5. Use of the te-form ... 2—A**

| V-te imasu |  *be ....ing*

This sentence pattern indicates that a certain action or motion is progressive.

Lee-san wa ima terebi o mite imasu.

*Mr. Lee is now watching television.*

**6. V-mashō ka**

This expression is used when the speaker is offering to do something to help the listener.

| Takushii o yobimashō ka. | *Shall I call a taxi?* |
| ··· Hai, yonde kudasai. | *··· Yes, please call one.* |

# Lesson 15

## 1. Use of the te-form . . . 3

V-te mo ii desu      *(You) may (do something.)*

This expression refers to permission.

        **Tabako o sutte mo ii desu.**       *You may smoke.*

When this sentence pattern is used in questions and answers, please be careful about the following usage.

1 ) **Kono kōjō de shashin o totte mo ii desu ka.**

        *May I take pictures in this factory?*

        ··· **Hai, ii desu.**           ··· *Yes, you may.*

        ··· **Iie, ikemasen.**         ··· *No, you must not.*

The answer in negative, "**Iie, ikemasen**", not only means to respond negatively to the request for permission, but implies prohibition i.e. *you must not do so.* Using this expression without knowing the context where it is allowed can be impolite.

2 ) Accordingly the following expression is used in a general individual relationship.

        **Anata no shashin o totte mo ii desu ka.** *May I take your picture?*

        ··· **Hai, dōzo. (ii desu yo.)**

          ··· *Yes, go ahead. (Please do so.)*

      ∗ ··· **Iie, chotto (komarimasu.)**        ··· *No, I don't quite (like it).*

∗ As there are different expressions for declining requests depending on the situation, you cannot learn them all here, but you are advised to be careful with these expressions.

## 2. Use of the te-form . . . 2—B

V-te imasu

In addition to the usage of "V-**te imasu**" that we learned in Lesson 14 (Use of the **te**-form . . . 2 — A), it is also used in describing a certain state or habit; that is, (1) when a state resulting from a certain action still remains, or (2) when the same action is repeatedly performed over a period of time.

     (1) **Suzuki-san wa mō kekkon-shite imasu.**

        *Mrs. Suzuki is already married.*

     (2) **Watashi wa jidōsha no kaisha de hataraite imasu.**

        *I work for an automobile company.*

3 . shirimasen (negative of **shitte imasu**)

       **Sentā no denwa-bangō o shitte imasu ka.**

       *Do you know the telephone number of the Center?*

     ··· **Hai, shitte imasu.**           ··· *Yes, I do.*

     ··· **Iie, shirimasen.**          ··· *No, I don't.*

The negative form of **shitte imasu** is **shirimasen.** Be careful not to say **shitte imasen.**

# Lesson 16

1 . **Joining sentences**

We have already learned that **soshite** and **to** are used to connect sentences and words respectively (lesson 8 and lesson 6). Here we will learn how to join coordinate sentences by using the inflection of words.

**Use of the te-form** ... 4

1 ) Verb sentences

| V-**te**,〜 V-**te**,〜 | *do..., and do...*

When two or more actions take place in succession, the actions are mentioned in the order of occurrence using the **te**-form. The tense of the sentence is determined by the tense form of the last verb in the sentence.

**Asa okite, gohan o tabete, kaisha e ikimasu.**

*In the morning I get up, have breakfast and then go to work.*

**Kinō Ginza e itte, tomodachi ni atte, eiga o mimashita.**

*Yesterday I went to Ginza, saw my friend and went to the movies.*

2 ) i-adjectives

| A-**kute**,〜 | *....and be....*

| ōki**i**   | → | ōki**kute**   |
| chiisa**i** | → | chiisa**kute** |
| i**i**(yo**i**) | → | yo**kute** |

**Tōkyō wa hito ga ōkute, nigiyaka desu.**

*Tokyo is heavily populated and bustling.*

3 ) Sentences ending with nouns or **na**-adjectives

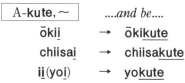

N<br>Na + **de**,〜     *..., and....*

When joining sentences that end with **desu** but are preceded by a noun or **na**-adjective, **desu** is changed to **de**.

**Rao-san wa Indo-jin de, Tōkyō-denki no kenshūsei desu.**

*Mr. Rao is an Indian and is a trainee of Tokyo Denki Co., Ltd.*

**Han-san wa kirei de, taihen shinsetsu desu.**

*Miss Han is beautiful and very kind.*

∗1 The above structures can be used not only for connecting sentences relating to the same theme but also sentences with different themes.

**Lee-san wa kikai o jisshū-shite, Han-san wa denki o
jisshū-shimasu.**

> *Mr. Lee is having practical training in machinery, and Miss Han is
> having practical training in electronics.*

**Rao-san wa Indo-jin de, Kimura-san wa Nihon-jin desu.**

> *Mr. Rao is Indian and Miss Kimura is Japanese.*

✱2 As with **soshite**, this method cannot connect words of contradictory no-
tion. In that case, **ga** is used.

✕ **Kono heya wa semakute, kirei desu.**

> *This room is small and clean.*

○ **Kono heya wa semai desu ga, kirei desu.**

> *This room is small but clean.*

## 2. Use of the te-form ... 5

> $V_1$-te kara, $V_2$      *after $V_1$..., ...$V_2$...*

This sentence pattern indicates that upon completion of the action denoted by
$V_1$, the action of $V_2$ is to be conducted.

**Shigoto ga owatte kara, sugu uchi e kaerimasu.**

> *After work is over, I will go home immediately.*

# Lesson 17

nai-form

The part of the words underlined below [before **nai** ] is called the **nai**-form.

1 . **How to make the nai-form**

(See p.138, **Renshū A, Dai 17 ka, SHIN NIHONGO NO KISO I**)

Group I (The vowel before -**masu** in the verbs of this group is always [-**i**] and is replaced by [-**a**] to make it a **nai**-form. Exceptions to this rule are **kaimasu**, where the **i** is replaced by **wa**, and such verbs as **hanashimasu** and **machimasu**, where **shi** and **chi** are replaced by **sa** and **ta** respectively.)

| | | |
|---|---|---|
| kakimasu | → | kakanai |
| yomimasu | → | yomanai |
| torimasu | → | toranai |
| kaimasu | → | kawanai |
| hanashimasu | → | hanasanai |
| machimasu | → | matanai |

Group II (The **nai**-form is the same as the **masu**-form)

| | | |
|---|---|---|
| tabemasu | → | tabenai |
| mimasu | → | minai |

Group III (The **nai**-form of **shimasu** is the same as the **masu**-form; **kimasu** becomes **konai**.)

| | | |
|---|---|---|
| benkyō-shimasu | → | benkyō-shinai |
| shimasu | → | shinai |
| kimasu | → | konai |

2 . **Use of the nai-form. . . 1**

| V-nai de kudasai | *Please do not*

cf. V-**te kudasai** *Please do....* (See Lesson14)

**Shashin o toranai de kudasai.** *Please do not take pictures.*

**3. Use of the nai-form ... 2**

| V-nakereba narimasen |     *(I) must ....*

This expression means something has to be done regardless of the will of the actor. Note that this is not a negative expression.

**Mainichi benkyō-shinakereba narimasen.**          *I must study everyday.*


**4. Use of the nai-form ... 3**

| V-nakute mo ii desu |     *(I) need not .... or (I) don't have to ....*

This sentence pattern indicates that the action described by the verb does not have to be done.

**Do-yōbi no gogo, benkyō-shinakute mo ii desu.**

*I don't have to study on Saturday afternoon.*


**5. Particle made ni**

**Made ni** indicates the point in time when an act or an action should be done by at the latest. That is, the point in time indicated by **made ni** is the time limit and the act or action is to be done before that time.

**Yoru 12-ji made ni Sentā e kaeranakereba narimasen.**

*(We) must go back to the Center by 12 o'clock at night.*

\* Make sure you do not confuse **made ni** with the particle **made** or the particle **ni** which we learned in Lesson 4.

①  **made**: indicates the point in time when the continuously performed act or action ends.

**Hiru 12-ji made Nihon-go o benkyō-shimasu.**

*(We) study Japanese until 12 o'clock noon.*

②  **ni**: indicates a point in time when a momentary action takes place.

**Asa 6-ji ni okimasu.**          *I get up at 6 o'clock in the morning.*

# Lesson 18

**Dictionary form**

This form is the basic form of a verb. Verbs are given in this form in the dictionary. ( cf. Lesson 20)

1. **How to construct the dictionary form**

    (See p.146, Renshū A, Dai 18 ka, SHIN NIHONGO NO KISO I)

    Group I

    | | | |
    |---|---|---|
    | kakimasu | → | kaku |
    | torimasu | → | toru |
    | kashimasu | → | kasu |
    | machimasu | → | matsu |

    Group II

    | | | |
    |---|---|---|
    | tabemasu | → | taberu |
    | mimasu | → | miru |

    Group III

    | | | |
    |---|---|---|
    | unten-shimasu | → | unten-suru |
    | shimasu | → | suru |
    | kimasu | → | kuru |

    \* shi and chi in **kashimasu** and **machimasu** become **su** and **tsu** respectively.

2. **How to use the dictionary form** ... 1

    > N
    > V-(r)u koto } ga dekimasu          *(I) can do ....*

    The verb which expresses possibility or ability is **dekimasu**. The subject of the ability or possibility, however, is indicated by attaching **ga** to a noun or a noun equivalent.

    1) Nouns

        When nouns are used, they should be nouns which describe an action (**unten, kaimono**, etc.,) as we learned in Lesson 13. Those nouns which refer to skills such as **Nihon-go** or **sukii** can also be used.

        | | |
        |---|---|
        | **Unten ga dekimasu.** | *I can drive.* |
        | **Nihon-go ga dekimasu.** | *I can speak Japanese.* |

41

2) Verbs

When expressing one's ability to do something (e.g., **yomimasu**), **koto** should be attached to the dictionary form (e.g., **yomu**) of the verb to make it a noun phrase and then **~ga dekimasu** is put after that.

**Lee-san wa <u>kanji o yomu koto</u> ga dekimasu.**

*Mr. Lee can read kanji.*

## 3. Meanings of dekimasu

**dekimasu** has two meanings.

1) Ability

**Lee-san wa kanji o yomu koto ga dekimasu.**

*Mr. Lee is able to read kanji.*

2) Possibility

**Uketsuke de takushii o yobu koto ga dekimasu.**

*You can call a taxi at the information desk.*

## 4. Use of the dictionary form ... 2

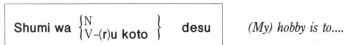

**Watashi no shumi wa e desu.**    *My hobby is painting.*

**Watashi no shumi wa e o miru koto desu.**

*My hobby is to look at paintings.*

When you cannot express the subject fully with a noun alone, you may use verb equivalents of nouns to refer to the activity and describe your hobby in a more concrete manner.

## 5. Use of the dictionary form ... 3

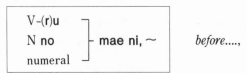

1) **~mae ni**, which refers to time before a given action, is attached to the dictionary form of a verb. It is always attached to the dictionary form both in the past and the future tenses.

**Nihon e kuru mae ni, Nihon-go o benkyō-shimashita.**

*I studied Japanese before I came to Japan.*

**Jisshū-suru mae ni, Nihon-go o benkyō-shimasu.**

*I will study Japanese before I have practical training.*

2) When **mae ni** comes after a noun, the particle **no** is put between the noun and **mae ni**.

**Kōgi no mae ni, chotto jimusho e kite kudasai.**

*Before the lecture, please come to the office for a while.*

When **mae ni** occurs after a numeral, the particle **no** is not necessary.

**3-nen no̶ mae ni kekkon-shimashita.**

*I married three years ago.*

# Lesson 19

ta-form

1. **How to construct the ta-form**

   The **ta**-form is made by replacing **te** and **de** of **te**-form verbs with **ta** and **da** respectively.

   | te-form | | ta-form |
   |---|---|---|
   | kaite | → | kaita |
   | nonde | → | nonda |
   | tabete | → | tabeta |
   | kite | → | kita |
   | shite | → | shita |

2. **Use of the ta-form... 1**

   V-ta koto ga arimasu    *(I) have (done)....*

   This sentence pattern is used in referring to something which one has experienced in the past.

   > **Nihon-ryōri o tabeta koto ga arimasu.**    *I have had Japanese food.*

   Note that it is, therefore, different from a sentence which merely states the fact that one did something at a certain time in the past.

   > **Senshū Nihon-ryōri o tabemashita.**    *I had Japanese food last week.*
   > **Watashi wa Indo kara kimashita.**    *I came from India.*

3. **Use of the ta-form... 2**

   V-ta + ri, V-ta + ri shimasu    *(I) do...and.., among other things.*

   We learned an expression for referring to some representative things among many (~ya ~ya) in Lesson 10. The sentences highlighted here are used in referring to some representative actions among many other activities. The tense of this sentence pattern is shown at the end of the sentence.

   > **Nichi-yōbi kaimono-shitari, eiga o mitari shimasu.**
   >
   > *On Sundays I go shopping and go to see movies among other things.*
   >
   > **Kinō kaimono-shitari, eiga o mitari shimashita.**
   >
   > *Yesterday I went shopping and went to see a movie among other things.*

**4.** ~narimasu

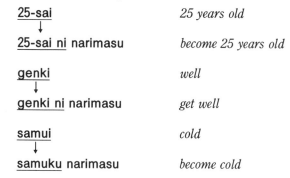

become....

**narimasu** indicates changes in a state or condition.

| | |
|---|---|
| <u>25-sai</u> ↓ | *25 years old* |
| <u>25-sai</u> ni narimasu | *become 25 years old* |
| <u>genki</u> ↓ | *well* |
| <u>genki</u> ni narimasu | *get well* |
| <u>samui</u> ↓ | *cold* |
| <u>samuku</u> narimasu | *become cold* |

**5. Use of the te-form** . . . 1-B

| V-te kudasai |  *Please do....*

We learned in Lesson 14 "V-**te kudasai**" as an expression for asking the listener to do something for the speaker. "V-**te kudasai**" that we learn in this lesson is an expression for encouraging or recommending the listener to do something.

Oishii desu yo. Dōzo takusan tabete kudasai.

*This is delicious. Please eat a lot.*

# Lesson 20

1. **Polite style of speech and plain style of speech**

   All the nouns, i-adjectives, na-adjectives and verbs used as the predicates of sentences in the examples so far have occurred at the end of the sentence accompanied by either **desu** or **-masu**. These predicates are in the polite-form and the sentences ending with these predicates are referred to as being in the polite style.

   Up to Lesson 19 we have learned various conjugations of verbs including the **nai**-form, dictionary form and **ta**-form. These forms are used with certain phrases as follows:

   | | |
   |---|---|
   | **tabetai desu.** | *I want to eat.* |
   | **taberu mae ni, te o araimasu.** | *I wash my hands before I eat.* |
   | **tabeta koto ga arimasu.** | *I have eaten* |

   These sentences also take **desu** or **-masu** at the end and are, therefore, in the polite style. Some **nai**-form or **ta**-form verbs and other verbs and adjectives without **desu** can occur at the end of sentences as predicates. These sentences which do not have **desu** or **-masu** and which have plain-form predicates at the end are referred to as being in the plain style.

   | | |
   |---|---|
   | **Ashita Tōkyō e iku.** | *I am going to Tokyo tomorrow.* |
   | **Mainichi isogashii.** | *I am busy everyday.* |
   | **Watashi wa Nihon-jin dewa nai.** | *I am not a Japanese.* |

   These plain style expressions are used in relaxed relationships such as among close friends and within a family. On the other hand, the polite style is used when talking to a person one has met for the first time, to one's superiors, or even to persons in a similar age group with whom one is not very close.

   * The plain style can be used even to a person one has met for the first time or to somebody who is slightly superior to you if you are socially or emotionally close to that person (when one feels a sense of intimacy with him or her), while the polite style is chosen if you are not very close to a person who is younger or lower in rank. Note that you need to know the interpersonal relationships of the Japanese very well to be able to tell when to use the plain style of speech. If the plain style is used inappropriately, you could sound rough and impolite.

## 2. Table of polite and plain forms

1) Polite style of speech and plain style of speech (See p.164. **Renshū A, Dai 20 ka, SHIN NIHONGO NO KISO I**)

|  | polite form | plain form |
|---|---|---|
| verb | kakimasu<br>kakimasen<br>kakimashita<br>kakimasendeshita | kaku (dictionary form)<br>kakanai (nai-form+nai)<br>kaita (ta-form)<br>kakanakatta<br>(nai-form+ nakatta) |
| i-adjective | atsui desu<br>atsukunai desu<br>atsukatta desu<br>atsukunakatta desu | atsui (desu omitted)<br>atsukunai<br>atsukatta<br>atsukunakatta |
| na-adjective<br>noun | hima desu<br>hima dewa arimasen<br>hima deshita<br>hima dewa arimasendeshita | hima da<br>hima dewa nai<br>hima datta<br>hima dewa nakatta |

2) Polite and plain forms of phrases which follow verbs
(See p.222, **Fōmu no tsukaikata, SHIN NIHONGO NO KISO I**)

| polite form | plain form | meaning | Lesson |
|---|---|---|---|
| nomitai desu<br>nomi ni ikimasu | nomitai<br>nomi ni iku | *(I) want to drink*<br>*(I) go to drink* | 13 |
| kaite kudasai<br>kaite imasu | kaite<br>kaite iru | *Please write*<br>*(I) am writing* | 14 |
| kaite mo ii desu<br>kakanakute mo ii<br>desu | kaite mo ii<br>kakanakute mo ii | *(you) may write*<br>*(you) do not have to write* | 15 |
| kaite agemasu<br>kaite moraimasu<br>kaite kuremasu | kaite ageru<br>kaite morau<br>kaite kureru | *(I) will write... for (you)*<br>*(I) have it written for (me)*<br>*(Somebody) writes... for (me)* | 24 |

| | | | |
|---|---|---|---|
| ikanakereba narimasen | ikanakereba naranai | *(I) must go* | 17 |
| ikanakute mo ii desu | ikanakute mo ii | *(I) do not have to go* | |
| taberu koto ga dekimasu | taberu koto ga dekiru | *(I) can eat* | 18 |
| taberu koto desu | taberu koto da | *(is) to eat* | |
| yonda koto ga arimasu | yonda koto ga aru | *(I) have read...* | 19 |
| yondari, kaitari shimasu | yondari, kaitari suru | *(I) read and write among others.* | |

When converting sentences connected by **kara** or **ga**, etc., into the plain style, all the polite forms in the sentence must be converted to the plain-form.

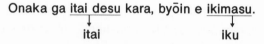

Onaka ga <u>itai desu</u> kara, byōin e <u>ikimasu</u>.

itai    iku

*As I have stomachache, I will go to the hospital.*

Nihon no tabemono wa <u>oishii desu</u> ga, <u>takai desu</u>.

oishii    takai

*Japanese food is good, but expensive.*

### 3. Questions in the plain style

Questions in the plain style generally omit the particle **ka**, which denotes a question, and end with a rising intonation, such as **nomu**↗ and **mita**↗, to indicate that the sentence is intended as a question.

    Kōhii o nomu?↗        *You want coffee?*

    ··· Un, nomu.↘        *··· Yeah, I do.*

There are plain style questions expressed with **ka**, such as **nomu ka** and **mita ka**, but this use is limited to between men and then only from a superior or senior to a younger or lower rank person, or between people in a very close relationship (such as from a father to his son, etc.).

In noun and adjective questions, **da**, which is the plain-form of **desu**, is omitted.

    Konban hima?        *Are you free tonight?*

    *··· Un, hima (da yo).        *··· Yeah, I am.*

    ··· Uun, hima dewa nai.        *··· No, I'm not free.*

48

··· Uun, hima ja nai.                  ··· *No, I'm not free.*

In conversation **dewa nai** often becomes **ja nai**.

\* In an answer in the affirmative, ending the sentence with a stressed **da** could sound too forceful. You may either omit **da** or add some sentence final particle to soften the tone of the sentence.

4 . **Plain-form of Hai and Iie**

     Hai → Un

     Iie → Uun (is spoken with the following accent; U͟u͟n͟)

       Iya or Iiya

5 . **Male language and female language**

In Japanese, men and women sometimes use different words. The conversation given above as an example in Lesson 20 was one between men. The latter part of the same conversation may be converted into one between women as follows:

    Suzuki: Kimura-san, ashita no ban hima?

               *Are you free tomorrow evening, Miss Kimura?*

    Kimura: Un, hima <u>yo</u>. Dōshite?   *Yes, I am. Why?*

    Suzuki: Pātii ni ikanai?        *Let's go to a party?*

    Kimura: Ii <u>wa</u> ne.          *Sounds great.*

          Basho wa doko?      *Where is it?*

    Suzuki: Fuji-hoteru. 6-ji goro hoteru no robii de matte iru <u>wa</u>.

               *At the Fuji Hotel. I'll be waiting for you in the lobby at around 6 o'clock.*

    Kimura: Wakatta <u>wa</u>. Ja, mata ashita.

           *Got you. Till tomorrow, then.*

# Lesson 21

**1. Particle to...3**

The ideas or information expressed with **omoimasu** and **iimasu** are indicated by the particle **to**.

> **Konban ame ga furu to omoimasu.**
>
> *I think that it will rain tonight.*
>
> **Kaisha no hito wa ashita Sentā e kuru to iimashita.**
>
> *The man from the company said he would come to the Center tomorrow.*

The particle **to** is preceded by the plain-form.

**2. ~ to omoimasu.** *I think that ....*

> plain-form + **to omoimasu**

This pattern is used in the following cases:

1) Conjecture

> **Konban ame ga furu to omoimasu.**
>
> *I think it will rain tonight.*
>
> \* **Rao-san wa Sentā ni inai to omoimasu.**
>
> *I think Mr. Rao is not in the Center.*
>
> **Tanaka-san wa mō uchi e kaetta to omoimasu.**
>
> *I think Mr. Tanaka has already gone home.*

\* **omoimasu** is not used in negative forms.

Instead the plain style part of the sentence preceding the particle **to** is made into a negative expression.

> ○ **Rao-san wa Sentā ni inai to omoimasu.**
>
> *I think Mr. Rao is not in the Center.*
>
> ✕ **Rao-san wa Sentā ni iru to omoimasen.**
>
> *I don't think Mr. Rao is in the Center.*

2) Stating one's opinion

> **Nihon wa kōtsū ga benri da to omoimasu.**
>
> *I think Japan has a convenient transportation system.*
>
> **Nihon wa hontō ni gijutsu ga susunde iru to omoimasu.**
>
> *I think Japanese technology is really advanced.*

50

### 3. Table of ～ to omoimasu and ～ to iimashita

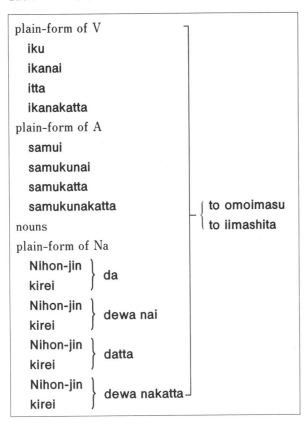

plain-form of V
  iku
  ikanai
  itta
  ikanakatta
plain-form of A
  samui
  samukunai
  samukatta
  samukunakatta
nouns
plain-form of Na

| Nihon-jin, kirei | } | da |
| Nihon-jin, kirei | } | dewa nai |
| Nihon-jin, kirei | } | datta |
| Nihon-jin, kirei | } | dewa nakatta |

{ to omoimasu
{ to iimashita

51

### 4. Omission of the particle to

When **omoimasu** and **iimashita** are used together with **sō** or **dō**, the particle **to** is omitted.

        Watashi mo sō omoimasu.     *I think so, too.*

        Nihon ni tsuite dō omoimasu ka.  *What do you think about Japan?*

5. ~ deshō.

When the speaker expects that the listener has some knowledge on the topic being discussed and that the listener will agree with the speaker's view, **deshō** is added to confirm the listener's agreement. **deshō** is preceded by the plain-form. However, for **na**-adjectives and nouns the plain-form **da** is replaced by **deshō**, e.g., nigiyaka da → nigiyaka deshō.

> **Do-yōbi Sentā de pātii ga aru deshō ↗?**
>
> *There is a party at the Center on Saturday, isn't there?*
>
> ··· **Hai, arimasu.**    ··· *Yes, there is.*
>
> **Shinjuku wa nigiyaka deshō ↗?**    *Shinjuku is bustling, isn't it?*
>
> ··· **Hai, nigiyaka desu.**    ··· *Yes, it is.*

# Lesson 22

### 1. Relative clause

| (Plain style sentence)　　N |
|---|

We have already learned how nouns or adjectives modify nouns (Lesson 2, Lesson 8). Plain style sentences with plain-form verbs can also modify nouns. A relative clause that modifies a noun always occurs before the word to be modified. Unlike English, relative pronouns are not necessary.

**Rao-san no kaisha**　　　　　　*Mr. Rao's company*

(noun　　**no** noun)

**ōkii　　kaisha**　　　　　　*big company*

(i-adjective noun)

**yūmeina　kaisha**　　　　　*famous company*

(**na**-adjective noun)

**Rao-san ga jisshū-suru kaisha**

(plain style　　　　　　noun)

　　*the company with which Mr. Rao will have practical training*

### 2. Particle ga which indicates the subject of a modifying clause

The particle **ga** instead of **wa** is used for the subject of a modifying clause.

**Rao-san wa jisshū-shimasu.**

　　*Mr. Rao will have practical training.*

**Rao-san ga jisshū-suru kaisha wa Tōkyō-denki desu.**

　　*The company with which Mr. Rao will have practical training is Tokyo Denki Co., Ltd.*

### 3. Examples of modifying clauses

1 )　| N　**wa**　modifying clause　N　**desu** |
|---|

**Kore wa watashi ga totta shashin desu.**

　　*This is the photo which I took.*

2 )　| modifying clause　N　**wa**　N　**desu** |
|---|

**Asoko ni iru hito wa Lee-san desu.**

　　*The person who is over there is Mr. Lee.*

**Senshū kengaku-shita tokoro wa Nagoya-jidōsha desu.**

　　*The place where we had practical training last week was Nagoya Motor Co., Ltd.*

3)

```
┌─────────────────────────────────────────────┐
│  modifying clause   N   wa  {Na}  desu        │
│                             {A }              │
└─────────────────────────────────────────────┘
```

**Kinō mita eiga wa totemo omoshirokatta desu.**

*The movie I saw yesterday was very interesting.*

4)

```
┌─────────────────────────────────────────────┐
│  modifying clause   N   {o }   V-masu         │
│                         {ga}                  │
└─────────────────────────────────────────────┘
```

**Jidōsha o tsukutte iru kōjō o kengaku-shimashita.**

*I visited a factory which manufactures automobiles.*

**Tomodachi ni au yakusoku ga arimasu.**

*I have an appointment to see a friend of mine.*

# Lesson 23

## 1. ~toki, ~

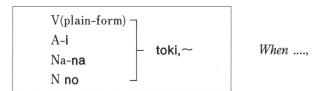

| V(plain-form) | | |
|---|---|---|
| A-**i** | | |
| Na-**na** | toki,~ | *When ....,* |
| N **no** | | |

**toki** connects two clauses and expresses the time when the state, or action described in the main clause which follows **toki** takes place. As shown in the table above, the forms of verbs, **i**-adjectives, **na**-adjectives and nouns connected to **toki** are the same as the forms when qualifying nouns.

> **Gaikoku e iku toki, pasupōto ga irimasu.**
>
> *When you go to a foreign country, you need a passport.*
>
> **Okane ga nai toki, tomodachi ni karimasu.**
>
> *When I don't have any money, I borrow some from my friend.*
>
> **Senshū Tōkyō e itta toki, kono shashin o torimashita.**
>
> *When I went to Tokyo last week, I took this picture.*
>
> **Isogashii toki, 10-ji goro made hatarakimasu.**
>
> *When I am busy, I work until around 10 o'clock.*
>
> **Himana toki, terebi o mitari, hon o yondari shimasu.**
>
> *When I am free, I watch television and read books, among other things.*
>
> **Gakusei no toki, yoku sukii ni ikimashita.**
>
> *When I was a student, I often went skiing.*

✳ The tense of a clause using **toki** is not influenced by the tense of the main clause which follows it, so *when I was young* or *when I was a child* in Japanese read as **wakai toki** or **kodomo no toki** respectively. You do not have to say **wakakatta toki** or **kodomo datta toki** in the past tense.

"V-**ta toki**" means completion of an action or state rather than being just a time reference. Thus, **Senshū Tōkyō e itta toki, kono shashin o torimashita** means *the photos were taken after arriving in Tokyo,* whereas, **Senshū Tōkyō e iku toki, kono shashin o torimashita** means that *the photos were taken on the way to Tokyo,* not after having been in Tokyo.

## 2. ~to, ~

| V-dictionary form ⎫ | | |
|---|---|---|
| V-nai-form + nai ⎭ | to, ~ | *If ...., then ....* |

When a situation inevitably triggers another situation, the necessary condition is indicated by **to** *if*.

**Kono botan o osu to, kikai ga ugokimasu.**

*If you press this button, the machine will start running.*

**Nihon-go ga wakaranai to, kōjō e itte, komarimasu.**

*If I don't understand Japanese, I will be in trouble when I go to the factory.*

**Kono michi o massugu iku to, migi ni eki ga arimasu.**

*If you go straight along this road, you will find the station on your right.*

✻ Expressions of one's will, hope, invitation or request cannot be used in the sentence which follows ~**to**.

✕　**Jikan ga aru to,**　┌**eiga o mi ni ikimasu.** (will)
　　*If I have time,*　　　│　*I will go to the movies.*
　　　　　　　　　　　└**eiga o mi ni ikitai desu.** (hope)
　　　　　　　　　　　　*I want to go to the movies.*

✕　**Jikan ga aru to,**　┌**eiga o mi ni ikimasen ka.** (invitation)
　　*If you have time,*　│　*won't you go to the movies?*
　　　　　　　　　　　└**chotto tetsudatte kudasai.** (request)
　　　　　　　　　　　　*please help me for a while.*

In those cases, the conditional expression ~**tara**, ~ is used instead of ~ **to**. (See Lesson 25)

## 3. Particle o ... 2

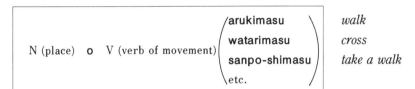

| N (place) | o | V (verb of movement) | arukimasu | walk |
| | | | watarimasu | cross |
| | | | sanpo-shimasu | take a walk |
| | | | etc. | |

We learned in Lesson 6 that the particle **o** is used to indicate the object of a transitive verb. The particle **o** is also used to denote the place where the action of a verb of movement, such as **arukimasu, watarimasu** and **sanpo-shimasu**, takes place.

**Hashi o watarimasu.**      *(I) cross the bridge.*

**Kōen o sanpo-shimasu.**      *I take a walk in the park.*

# Lesson 24

1. **Verbs for giving and receiving**

   Verbs which express an act of giving or receiving are called conferment verbs. In addition to **agemasu** *to give* and **moraimasu** *to receive,* which we learned in Lesson 7, we also have **kuremasu** *to give* as one of the conferment verbs in Japanese.

   | N o kuremasu | *to give*

   We learned that **agemasu** means *to give* in Lesson 7, but this cannot be used in the context of where somebody else gives something to the speaker. In this case **kuremasu** is used.

   > **Watashi wa Lee-san ni shatsu o agemashita.**
   >
   > *I gave Mr. Lee a shirt.*
   >
   > ✕ **Ali-san wa watashi ni shatsu o agemashita.**
   >
   > **Ali-san wa watashi ni shatsu o kuremashita.**
   >
   > *Mr. Ali gave me a shirt.*

   There are other conferment verbs such as **yarimasu, kudasaimasu** and **itadakimasu** which are not covered by this textbook.

2. **Conferment expressions**

   **agemasu, moraimasu** and **kuremasu** are all used in expressing the giving and taking of things. These verbs are also used to refer to motions. They indicate the direction of the act in terms of who is doing that act for whom, while also expressing a sense of good will or gratitude. In this case the act is expressed by the **te**-form of a verb.

   1) | V-**te agemasu** | *do something for somebody (by way of doing a favor)*

   > **Watashi wa Kimura-san ni kasa o kashite agemashita.**
   >
   > *I lent Miss Kimura an umbrella.*
   >
   > **Nimotsu o motte agemashō ka.**
   >
   > *Shall I carry your baggage for you?*

   In this context one does something for somebody with a sense of goodwill. When the speaker is the actor, the act of doing a favor could give an impression of forcing upon the beneficiary unwanted help. You are, therefore, advised to avoid using this expression to somebody who you do not know very well and who is senior or superior to you. You may use it to somebody with whom you have a very close, friendly relationship.

When one offers an act of goodwill or assistance to somebody who is not very close, "V-**mashō ka**" (See Lesson 14) is used.

| | |
|---|---|
| **Takushii o yobimashō ka.** | *Shall I call a taxi for you?* |
| **Tetsudaimashō ka.** | *May I help you?* |

2) | V-**te moraimasu** |   *(I) have somebody do something for (me),* or *somebody kindly does something for (me).*

**Watashi wa Suzuki-san ni Nihon-go o oshiete moraimashita.**

*Mrs. Suzuki kindly taught me Japanese.*

This expression conveys a sense of gratitude on the part of those who receive a favor.

3) | V-**te kuremasu** |   *(Somebody) does a favor for* (me)

**Kanai wa (watashi ni) kodomo no shashin o okutte kuremashita.**

*My wife has sent me photos of my children.*

Like "V-**te moraimasu**", this expression also conveys a sense of gratitude on the part of those who receive a favor. The difference is that "V-**te moraimasu**" has the receiver of the act as the subject of the sentence, while "V-**te kuremasu**" has the actor as the subject of the sentence, implying the actor (the subject) voluntarily takes the action. The receiver of the act in the latter is often the speaker and **watashi ni**, which indicates the receiver, is often omitted.

# Lesson 25

## 1. Conditional expressions

### 1) Conditional form

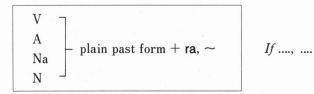

$$\left.\begin{array}{l} \text{V} \\ \text{A} \\ \text{Na} \\ \text{N} \end{array}\right\} \text{plain past form} + \textbf{ra}, \sim \qquad \textit{If ...., ....}$$

When **ra** is attached to the past tense plain form of verbs, adjectives, etc., it changes the preceding clause into a conditional expression. When a speaker wants to state his or her opinion, situation, request, etc., in the conditional, this pattern is used.

**Ame ga futtara, pikunikku ni ikimasen.**

*If it rains, I will not go to the picnic.*

**Jikan ga nakattara, pātii ni ikimasen.**

*If I don't have time, I will not go to the party.*

**Yasukattara, bideo o kaimasu.**

*If it is inexpensive, I will buy a video tape recorder.*

**Hima dattara, Tōkyō-tawā e ikimasu.**

*If I am free, I will go to the Tokyo Tower.*

**Ame dattara, uchi ni imasu.**

*If it rains, I will stay home.*

### 2) V-**tara**, ∼   *when ...., if...,*

This pattern is used to describe a condition when an action or state described by the verb is achieved or accomplished, then what is described in the main clause will happen.

**Nan-ji goro kengaku ni ikimasu ka.**

*About what time are we leaving for the plant visit?*

··· **Hirugohan o tabetara, sugu ikimasu.**

··· *We will leave as soon as we finish lunch.*

## 2. Expression for reverse supposition

$$\left.\begin{array}{l} \text{V-te} \\ \text{A-kute} \\ \text{Na} \\ \text{N} \end{array}\right\} \text{de} \Big] + \text{mo,}\sim \qquad \textit{Even if ..., ... or Even though...,...}$$

**mo** is attached to the **te**-form to construct a word which presents a reverse condition. Contrary to "~**tara**,~", this expression is used when an event which is expected to happen naturally under the given circumstances does not materialize or when the outcome is contrary to what is expected.

**Suitchi o irete mo, kikai ga ugokimasen.**
> *Even though I turn on the switch, the machine does not work.*

**Takakute mo, kono rajikase o kaitai desu.**
> *Even if it is expensive, I want to buy this radio-cassette recorder.*

**Shizuka demo, neru koto ga dekimasen.**
> *Even if it is quiet, I cannot sleep.*

**Nichi-yōbi demo, shigoto o shimasu.**
> *Even if it is Sunday, I work.*

## 3. Moshi and Ikura

**Moshi** and **Ikura** are used in a sentence with "~**tara**" and "~**te mo,** ~" respectively, to indicate that the sentence is going to present a condition. **Moshi** implies that an emphasis is on the speaker's supposition, while **Ikura** is meant to stress the degree of conditionality.

**Moshi ame ga futtara, pikunikku ni ikimasen.**
> *If it rains, I will not go to the picnic.*

**Ikura takakute mo, kono rajikase o kaitai desu.**
> *However expensive it may be, I want to buy this radio cassette recorder.*

## 4. ⬛ Sentence **ne** ⬛ ...2

The particle **ne** is used by the speaker to seek agreement or approval from the listener and is similar in function to such English structures as *isn't it?*, *aren't you?* etc.

**Ashita wa pikunikku desu ne.**
> *Tomorrow we are going on a picnic, aren't we?*

··· **Hai, sō desu.** ··· *Yes, that's right.*

# Particles

## 1. [wa]

A : **wa** is attached to a noun or its equivalent word or phrase and indicates the main topic of a sentence. Its influence extends all the way to the end of the sentence, thus holding the sentence together.

       **Kore wa watashi ga totta shashin desu.**    *This is the photo that I took.*

B : **wa** is capable of highlighting various words it holds at the beginning of the sentence and makes them the main topic.

① { **Ima isogashii desu.**            *I am busy now.*
     { **Ima wa isogashii desu.**       *Now, I am busy.*

     { **Kinō doko mo ikimasendeshita.**    *I didn't go anywhere yesterday.*
     { **Kinō wa doko mo ikimasendeshita.**  *Yesterday I didn't go anywhere.*

     If there is no particle immediately after the word to be highlighted, **wa** is placed in that position.

② { **Koko ni hon ga arimasu.**       *Here is a book.*
     { **Hon wa koko ni arimasu.**      *The book is here.*

     { **Kinō kono shatsu o kaimashita.**   *Yesterday I bought this shirt.*
     { **Kono shatsu wa kinō kaimashita.**  *This shirt, I bought it yesterday.*

     If the particle **ga** or **o** immediately follows the word to be highlighted, it is replaced by **wa**.

③ { **Koko de kitte o utte imasu.**     *Stamps are sold here.*
     { **Koko de wa kitte o utte imasu.**  *Here stamps are sold.*

     { **Tōkyō ni taishikan ga arimasu.**   *The embassy is located in Tokyo.*
     { **Tōkyō ni wa taishikan ga arimasu.**  *In Tokyo the embassy is located.*

     { **Ashita Hiroshima e ikimasu.**     *Tomorrow I go to Hiroshima.*
     { **Hiroshima (e) wa ashita ikimasu.**  *I go to Hiroshima tomorrow.*

     If there is a particle **de**, **ni** or **e**, etc., following the word to be highlighted, **wa** is placed after it. **e** may be omitted, leaving only **wa** after the highlighted word.

## 2. [mo]

A : Like **wa**, **mo** also highlights various words or events and makes them the main topic of a sentence; the difference is that **mo** is used when the matter to be referred to with **mo** is presupposed.

**Ano hito wa kenshūsei desu. Watashi mo kenshūsei desu.**

*He is a trainee. I am a trainee, too.*

\* Note that **mo** does not occur independently at the beginning or end of a sentence.

B : When **mo** is preceded by an interrogative in a sentence which has a negative predicate, **mo** does not denote a question but implies a complete negative.

**Ashita doko mo ikimasen.**     *I am not going anywhere tomorrow.*

## 3. [no]

**no** connects a noun with another noun or its equivalent word or phrase when the first word qualifies the latter to produce various meanings (except for D below).

A : Affiliation, possession, attributes, etc.

**Watashi wa Indo no Rao desu.**     *I am Rao from India.*

**Kore wa watashi no hon desu.**     *This is my book.*

**NTC wa konpyūtā no kaisha desu.**     *NTC is a computer company.*

B : When **no** is preceded by a noun which describes an action or motion or a noun derived from a verb, **no** indicates the object of the action represented by the noun.

**Taipu no tsukai-kata o oshiete kudasai.**

*Please tell me how to use a typewriter.*

C : **no** indicates a point in time or a position in space.

**Kinō no ban benkyō-shimashita ka.** *Did you study last night?*

**Tsukue no ue ni hon ga arimasu.**     *There is a book on the desk.*

D : ( 1 ) **no** indicates somebody's possession.

**Kono hon wa watashi no desu.**     *This book is mine.*

( 2 ) **no** means a "thing".

**Chiisai no o misete kudasai.**     *Please show me a smaller one.*

## 4. [o]

A : **o** indicates the object of a transitive verb.

**Gohan o tabemasu.**     *(I) eat a meal.*

C : When **o** is used with a verb which relates to leaving or departing, such as **demasu** and **orimasu**, it indicates a starting point or a departure point.

**Heya o demasu.**     *I leave the room.*

D : When **o** is used with a verb relating to movement, such as **sanpo-shimasu, watarimasu, arukimasu** and **ikimasu**, etc., it indicates the place which is passed.

**Kōen o sanpo-shimasu.**     *I take a walk in the park.*

63

## 5. 〔ga〕

A : ( 1 ) When **ga** is used with adjectives or verbs that denote one's preference or wish, such as **suki, kirai, hoshii, -tai,** etc., the object of the desire or preference is indicated by **ga**.

> **Watashi wa ringo ga suki desu.**      *I like apples.*
> **Watashi wa kamera ga hoshii desu.**      *I want a camera.*

( 2 ) When **ga** is used with verbs of possession, such as **arimasu** and **imasu**, or with verbs or adjectives that denote one's ability, the object of the predicate is indicated by **ga**.

> **Watashi wa kodomo ga futari imasu.**      *I have two children.*
> **Watashi wa Nihon-go ga wakarimasu.**      *I can understand Japanese.*

B : When the topic of a statement is first mentioned, and then a description is made concerning the topic, the particle **wa** indicates the topic or theme and **ga** indicates the subject of the description.

> **Watashi wa atama ga itai desu.**      *I have a headache.*

C : When a scene or the existence of someone is being described with **arimasu** or **imasu**, the subject is marked with **ga**.

> **Asoko ni otoko no hito ga imasu.**      *There is a man over there.*
> **Asoko ni ginkō ga arimasu.**      *There is a bank over there.*

D : **ga** indicates the object of comparison in a comparative sentence.

> **Shinkansen to hikōki to, dochira ga hayai desu ka.**
> *Which is faster, Shinkansen or airplane?*
> ··· **Hikōki no hō ga hayai desu.**      ··· *Airplane is faster.*

E : In describing a phenomenon itself, or in describing a phenomenon upon noticing it, the subject of that motion or action is indicated by **ga**.

> **Ame ga futte imasu.**      *It is raining.*

F : The subject of a subordinate clause is denoted by **ga**.

> **Kore wa watashi ga totta shashin desu.**
> *This is the photo that I took.*

G : The particle **wa** has the function of denoting the theme of a statement and is used to discuss how the main theme presented by **wa** evolves, while the particle **ga** introduces the subject of the predicate. Therefore, when the subject is interrogative, **ga** is the particle which follows it.

> **Ali-san ga kono shatsu o kuremashita.**
> *Mr. Ali gave me this shirt.*
> **Kinō dare ga kimashita ka.**      *Who came yesterday?*

## 6. 〔ni〕

A : **ni** is placed after a noun that denotes time and indicates the point in time when an action or motion is performed.

    **Maiasa 6-ji ni okimasu.**      *Every morning I get up at 6 o'clock.*

B : **ni** indicates the person or place which is an object to whom or to which the action or motion is directed.

    **Watashi wa tomodachi ni hon o agemashita.**

        *I gave my friend a book.*

C : **ni** is used together with verbs relating to receiving something, such as **moraimasu** and **naraimasu**, etc., to indicate the source of the thing to be received.

    **Watashi wa Katō-san ni tokei o moraimashita.**

        *I was given a watch by Mr. Kato.*

D : **ni** is used together with verbs which relate to existence, such as **arimasu** and **imasu**, etc., to indicate the place where the person(s) or thing(s) is (are).

    **Tanaka-san wa jimusho ni imasu.**      *Mr. Tanaka is in the office.*

E : **ni** is used together with verbs such as **hairimasu, suwarimasu** and **norimasu** etc., to indicate the arriving point or destination.

    **Heya ni hairimasu.**      *I enter the room.*

F : When **ni** precedes verbs which refer to moving toward somewhere, such as **ikimasu, kimasu** and **kaerimasu**, etc., it denotes the purpose of the move.

    **Sukii ni ikimasu.**      *I am going to go skiing.*

    **Depāto e kutsu o kai ni ikimasu.**

        *I am going to the department store to buy shoes.*

G : **ni** is used together with verbs relating to changes or transformation, such as **kaemasu** and **narimasu**, etc., to indicate the outcome of the change.

    **Doru o en ni kaemasu.**      *I change the dollars to yen.*

## 7. 〔e〕

When **e** is used after a noun which denotes a place and is followed by a verb of movement, such as **ikimasu, kimasu,** and **kaerimasu**, etc., it indicates the direction of the move.

    **Kyōto e ikimasu.**      *I will go to Kyoto.*

\*In the above sentence, the particle **ni**, which indicates an arrival point, is sometimes used.

    **Kyōto ni ikimasu.**      *I will go to Kyoto.*

## 8. [de]

A : **de** indicates a means, method, tool, etc., used in performing an action or motion.

**Densha de Tōkyō e ikimasu.**     *I will go to Tokyo by train.*

B : **de** indicates the place where an action or motion is performed.

**Depāto de shatsu o kaimasu.**

*I will buy a shirt at the department store.*

C : **de** indicates the scope of choice when choosing one out of an entire group.

**Kurasu de Narong-san ga ichiban wakai desu.**

*Mr. Narong is the youngest in the class.*

## 9. [to]

A : **to** denotes a partner with whom an action is done.

**Watashi wa tomodachi to Tōkyō e ikimasu.**

*I will go to Tokyo with my friend.*

B : **to** connect nouns in coordinate relation.

**Pan to tamago o tabemasu.**     *I eat bread and eggs.*

C : In a sentence which compares specific items, **to** indicates the objects of comparison.

**Kōhii to kōcha to, dochira ga ii desu ka.**

*Which would you like, coffee or tea?*

## 10. [ya]

Like **to**, **ya** is used in connecting nouns. The difference is that **to** enumerates, while **ya** refers to only two or three representative items.

**Heya ni beddo ya tsukue ya isu ga arimasu.**

*There is a bed, a desk and a chair among other things in the room.*

## 11. [kara] [made]

**kara** and **made** show the starting point and the ending point respectively.

**Mainichi 9-ji kara 5-ji made hatarakimasu.**

*Everyday I work from 9 to 5.*

**Tōkyō kara Ōsaka made shinkansen de 3-jikan gurai kakarimasu.**

*It takes about 3 hours by Shinkansen to go from Tokyo to Osaka.*

## 12. [made ni]

**made ni** indicates the point in time when the action or motion is to be conducted by at the latest. That is, the point in time indicated by **made ni** is the time limit and the action must be done not later than that time.

12-ji made ni Sentā e kaeranakereba narimasen.

*I must go back to the Center by 12 o'clock.*

## 13. [ka]

A : **ka** is placed at the end of a sentence to make it a question.

    **Anata wa Rao-san desu ka.**     *Are you Mr. Rao?*

B : ( 1 ) **ka** is used to confirm what the other person said.

    **Kaban-uriba wa doko desu ka.**     *Where is the bag department?*

    ··· **Kaban-uriba desu ka. 5-kai desu.**

        *··· The bag department? It's on the 5th floor.*

( 2 ) **ka** is uttered with a falling intonation to indicate the speaker is considering what has been said or to express exclamation.

    **Nihon-go no benkyō wa 9-ji kara desu.**

    *The Japanese language class begins at 9 o'clock.*

    ··· **Sō desu ka.**     *··· Is that so.*

## 14. [yori]

**yori** indicates the reference used for comparison in a comparative sentence.

    **Indo wa Nihon yori atsui desu.**     *India is hotter than Japan.*

## 15. [ne]

1 ) **ne** is placed at the end of a sentence to appeal to the listener for agreement or in anticipation of the listener's consent. (It is not used in a monologue.)

    **Benkyō wa 9-ji kara 5-ji made desu.**

    *The class is from 9 o'clock to 5 o'clock.*

    ··· **Sō desu ka. Taihen desu ne.**     *··· Is that so. That must be hard.*

    **Kireina kōen desu ne.**     *This is a beautiful park, isn't it?*

    ··· **Sō desu ne.**     *··· Yes, isn't it?*

2 ) When **ne** is used in **Ii desu ne**, it implies acceptance of an invitation or proposal.

    **Issho ni eiga o mimasen ka.**     *Won't you go to the movies with me?*

    ··· **Ii desu ne.**     *··· That sounds good.*

    **Ashita Fujisan e ikimasu.**     *I am going to Mt. Fuji tomorrow.*

    ＊··· **Ii desu ne.**     *··· That is nice.*

  ＊In this case the listener is not invited to go, so the meaning here is the same as with 1 ) above.

3 ) When **sō desu ne** is the answer to a question, invitation, suggestion, etc., it implies that the speaker is thinking rather than responding immediately. In this context, the pronunciation of **ne** is slightly lengthened.

Nihon-go no benkyō wa dō desu ka.

*How is your Japanese language study?*

··· Sō desu ne. Muzukashii desu ga, omoshiroi desu.

··· *Well, it is difficult, but interesting.*

Kireina kōen desu ne.          *This is a beautiful park, isn't it?*

＊··· Sō desu ne.                    ··· *That's right.*

＊Sō desu ne here indicates consent to a question which is seeking the listener's agreement (See 1) above). In this case ne is not pronounced with a long 'e' sound.

**16.** 〔yo〕

yo is placed at the end of a sentence to state emphatically and decisively what the listener doesn't know or what the speaker believes.

Kono densha wa Yokohama e ikimasu ka.

*Does this train go to Yokohama?*

··· Iie, ikimasen. 3-bansen desu yo.

··· *No, it doesn't. That's on platform No.3.*

新 日 本 語 の 基 礎 I
文 法 解 説 書 英 語 版

1992 年 4 月 1 日　初版第 1 刷発行
2002 年 3 月 14 日　第 11 刷 発 行

編　集　　財団法人　海外技術者研修協会
発行者　　小川　巖
発　行　　株式会社　スリーエーネットワーク
　　　　　〒101-0064 東京都千代田区猿楽町 2 - 6 - 3 （松栄ビル）
　　　　　電話　営業 03 (3292) 5751
　　　　　　　　編集 03 (3292) 6521
　　　　　http://www.3anet.co.jp
印　刷　　株式会社　創英

# ❖実践が生んだ短期集中日本語教材「新日本語の基礎」シリーズ❖

| | | | |
|---|---|---|---|
| 新日本語の基礎Ⅰ　本冊 | | 新日本語の基礎Ⅰ　標準問題集 | 825円 |
| 　漢字かなまじり版 | 2,505円 | 新日本語の基礎Ⅱ　標準問題集 | 874円 |
| 　ローマ字版 | 2,505円 | しんにほんごのきそ　かな練習帳 | |
| 新日本語の基礎Ⅰ　分冊 | | 　英語版 | 680円 |
| 　英語訳 | 1,505円 | 　中国語版 | 680円 |
| 　中国語訳 | 1,505円 | 　スペイン語版 | 680円 |
| 　タイ語訳 | 1,505円 | 　ポルトガル語版 | 680円 |
| 　インドネシア語訳 | 1,505円 | 新日本語の基礎　漢字練習帳Ⅰ | |
| 　スペイン語訳 | 1,505円 | 　英語版 | 1,748円 |
| 　韓国語訳 | 1,505円 | 　スペイン語版 | 1,748円 |
| 　ポルトガル語訳 | 1,505円 | 　ポルトガル語版 | 1,748円 |
| 　ロシア語訳 | 1,505円 | 新日本語の基礎　漢字練習帳Ⅱ | |
| 　ベトナム語訳 | 1,505円 | 　英語版 | 1,748円 |
| 　フランス語訳 | 1,505円 | 　スペイン語版 | 1,748円 |
| 　ビルマ語訳 | 1,505円 | 　ポルトガル語版 | 1,748円 |
| 新日本語の基礎Ⅰ　文法解説書 | | | |
| 　英語版 | 1,650円 | 新日本語の基礎Ⅰ　教師用指導書 | 2,718円 |
| 　中国語版 | 1,650円 | 新日本語の基礎Ⅱ　教師用指導書 | 2,718円 |
| 　タイ語版 | 1,650円 | 日本語の教え方の秘訣　上 | 2,913円 |
| 　インドネシア語版 | 1,650円 | 日本語の教え方の秘訣　下 | 2,913円 |
| 　スペイン語版 | 1,650円 | 続・日本語の教え方の秘訣　上 | 2,427円 |
| 　韓国語版 | 1,650円 | 続・日本語の教え方の秘訣　下 | 2,427円 |
| 　ポルトガル語版 | 1,650円 | クラス活動集101 | 1,748円 |
| 　ロシア語版 | 1,650円 | 続・クラス活動集131 | 2,039円 |
| 　ベトナム語版 | 1,650円 | | |
| 　フランス語版 | 1,650円 | 新絵教材（カラー） | 58,252円 |
| 新日本語の基礎Ⅱ　本冊 | | 新絵教材Ⅱ（カラー） | 116,505円 |
| 　漢字かなまじり版 | 2,524円 | 新絵教材Ⅱ（白黒） | 36,893円 |
| 　ローマ字版 | 2,524円 | 携帯用新絵教材（白黒） | 5,631円 |
| 新日本語の基礎Ⅱ　分冊 | | 携帯用新絵教材Ⅱ（白黒） | 5,600円 |
| 　英語訳 | 1,553円 | 新日本語の基礎Ⅰ | |
| 　中国語訳 | 1,553円 | 　会話・練習Cイラストシート | 9,709円 |
| 　タイ語訳 | 1,553円 | 新日本語の基礎Ⅰ　カセットテープ新装版 | 7,000円 |
| 　インドネシア語訳 | 1,553円 | 新日本語の基礎Ⅱ　カセットテープ新装版 | 7,000円 |
| 　スペイン語訳 | 1,553円 | 新日本語の基礎Ⅰ　CD | 8,000円 |
| 　韓国語訳 | 1,553円 | 新日本語の基礎Ⅱ　CD | 7,000円 |
| 　ポルトガル語訳 | 1,553円 | 新日本語の基礎Ⅰ　会話ビデオ NTSC | 10,000円 |
| 　ロシア語訳 | 1,553円 | 新日本語の基礎Ⅰ　会話ビデオ PAL | 17,000円 |
| 　ベトナム語訳 | 1,553円 | 新日本語の基礎Ⅱ　会話ビデオ NTSC | 10,000円 |
| 　フランス語訳 | 1,553円 | 新日本語の基礎Ⅱ　会話ビデオ PAL | 17,000円 |
| 　ビルマ語訳 | 1,553円 | 新日本語の基礎Ⅰ　復習ビデオ NTSC | 10,000円 |
| 新日本語の基礎Ⅱ　文法解説書 | | 新日本語の基礎Ⅰ　復習ビデオ PAL | 17,000円 |
| 　英語版 | 1,748円 | 新日本語の基礎Ⅱ　復習ビデオ NTSC | 12,000円 |
| 　中国語版 | 1,748円 | 新日本語の基礎Ⅱ　復習ビデオ PAL | 19,000円 |
| 　タイ語版 | 1,748円 | | |
| 　インドネシア語版 | 1,748円 | | |
| 　スペイン語版 | 1,748円 | ホームページで新刊や日本語セミナーを | |
| 　韓国語版 | 1,748円 | ご案内しております | |
| 　ポルトガル語版 | 1,748円 | http://www.3anet.co.jp | |
| 　ロシア語版 | 1,748円 | | |
| 　ベトナム語版 | 1,748円 | | |
| 　フランス語版 | 1,748円 | スリーエーネットワーク | 価格は税別です |